LET'S PLAY CHECKERS

By

KENNETH M. GROVER

RUNNER-UP TENTH AMERICAN TOURNEY,
U. S. ELEVEN MEN BALLOT CHAMPION

And

TOMMIE WISWELL

NOTED PROBLEMIST AND FORMER
NEW YORK CITY TITLE-HOLDER

A PROGRESSIVE GUIDE FOR THE STUDENT

ISHI PRESS
INTERNATIONAL

Let's Play Checkers
by Kenneth M. Grover
and Thomas Wiswell

First Published in 1940 by David McKay

This Printing in October, 2016
by Ishi Press in New York and Tokyo
with a new introduction by Sam Sloan

ISBN 4-87187-747-7
978-4-87187-747-3

Ishi Press International
1664 Davidson Avenue, Suite 1B
Bronx NY 10453-7877
USA
1-917-507-7226
1-917-659-3397
samhsloan@gmail.com
Printed in the United States of America

Introduction by Sam Sloan

Let's Play Checkers
by Kenneth M. Grover
and Thomas Wiswell
Introduction by Sam Sloan

This is regarded as one of the best books for the average player ever written. This modern textbook pays particular attention to the many problems confronting the average player. Besides an extensive game collection that shows the best restrictive lines for Black and White (thus reducing study to a minimum) it includes a new method for studying the Mid-Game.

This is an enlightening discussion of the major midgame formations and the art of transportation. Many model three move games as played by America's foremost masters with many new lines of play. (Three move restriction is played by all the experts and is fully explained.) Many brilliant endgame themes every player should know. 100 selected problems by America's foremost composers. Latest revised rules for match and tourney play. And numerous other features of interest to all grades of players.

Checkers is probably the world's best known board game. In America, more than 100 million people have played at least one game of checkers. In England, the game is known as Draughts. There are around 150 varieties. In America, most African-Americans play Spanish checkers or "pool", which features flying kings. In Eastern Europe and Holland, checkers is played on a 10x10 board. In Canada, it is sometimes played on a 12x12 board.

First published in 1940, this book is concerned with Go As You Please or GAYP Free-Style Standard

Introduction by Sam Sloan

American Checkers.

The authors were two of Americas foremost Checkerists. Both won numerous titles and important games during their brilliant and checkered careers. - They start the reader off “at scratch” and with patience and understanding take him along the road that ultimately leads to the goal of practically every checker player – the expert class.

Kenneth M. Grover

A complete list of the many titles and matches won by Mr. Grover would take up more space than is available here. His outstanding titles are United States Eleven Man Ballot Champion (since 1937) and ranking number two player in America (Runner up to Asa Long, the world's champion in 1939 American Championships.) The leading players whom he met in match or tourney play include Asa Long, World's Champion, Willie Ryan, National Checker Association Champion, Walter Hallman, Former U.S. Junior Champion, H. B. Reynolds, Internationalist, Arthur Reisman, former Michigan Champion; Ray Gould, Champion of New England, and Jesse B. Hanson, Pacific Coast Titleholder – Champions All! He made several transcontinental tours giving brilliant simultaneous and blindfold exhibitions of his skill at checkers.

Thomas M. Wiswell

Besides being a noted player and writer of the game, Mr. Wiswell earned for himself the reputation of being America's leading problem composer. His achievements include first price in the 1938 New York Master's Tournament and being topped only by Ryan and

Introduction by Sam Sloan

Grover in the 1940 Empire State Event. He won major prizes. Although Let's Play Checkers was Mr. Wiswell's first book, he was the author of many newspaper and magazine articles on the game that have been widely read and discussed.

I Sam Sloan met Ken Grover at the Chess Friends of Northern California Money Tournament in Oakland California in 1963, in the first round when he was playing at the board next to mine. This was known as the "Chess Friends Money Tournament", so called because it was the only Chess Friends tournament with cash prize money.

In the first round of chess tournaments, the top rated players play the bottom rated players. I had been paired up because my rating was low as my recent results had not been rated yet. In the first round, I was paired against Col. Edmond Edmundson who later became USCF Executive director. Edmondson had been given a rating of 2000. I quickly discovered that this was an honorary rating as I defeated him easily. His real strength was probably no more than 1700.

Grover was playing on the board next to me. What I saw was an impressively looking and obviously intelligent young man playing against an old codger. I did not know either of them so I was trying to figure out which one was the weak player and which one was the strong player. As they quickly drew his first game, I got no information about this.

In the last round, I was shocked to see the old codger Ken Grover playing on board one against National Master Peter Cleghorn. After drawing his first round game, Grover had wiped out his remaining opponents and was now contesting the top prize. He won that tournament by defeating International Master Peter Cleghorn in the last round and won the money, a shocking upset since nobody in the Bay Area knew him.

He had just arrived in the Bay Area after living in Seattle Washington. Cleghorn later referred to Grover as "a master".

As I recall, Grover said he had recently arrived in the Bay Area from Seattle. It became apparent that Grover had played the "Swiss Gambit". By drawing his first round game, Grover would play against weaker opponents in the later rounds. Meanwhile, the top players would knock each other out playing against each other.

Later, Grover played in another tournament, this time in Marin County. This time he drew his first round game and then lost all the rest. I concluded that he wanted to get his rating down so he could qualify for class prizes in later events. However, this did not work because the USCF's rating office did not realize that the winner of the first tournament had finished last in the second tournament, so rated them as two separate players.

His third tournament was the 3rd Hamilton Air Force Base Open April 26-28, 1963. In my reprint of California Chess Reporter 1961-1964 ISBN 4871875547 page 266 it shows that Ken Grover won the 3rd Hamilton Air Force Base Open. This was a strong tournament. Grover defeated Masters Henry Gross and John Blackstone, after again drawing an early game against a much weaker opponent.

Ken Grover became a professional poker player at

the Oaks Club in Emeryville, California. He played there every day. I often played there too and we had many discussions about chess and checkers. That is where I got to know him.

In December 1967, I moved to New York and never saw him after that, as I did not return to California for 14 years.

Larry Parr published a fascinating article about Ken Grover and Chess Grandmaster Arthur Dake. He said that Grover and Dake shared a room and a bed together off the boardwalk in Coney Island in Brooklyn New York where they made their living during the depression in the 1930s playing chess and checkers for quarters with visitors to the beach. Before he became a famous actor, Humphrey Bogart played there too.

Here is the article I was remembering. It was posted in July 2009. Unfortunately, the author, Larry Parr, is dead now.

> "Gentlemen,
>
> "Art Dake lived in NYC with Ken Grover on 6th and 52 St. in the late 1920s and early 1930s. They took cuts from poker games running in their apartment.
>
> "One day six thugs with "heaters" arrived, and they got out of the poker business. They later went out to Coney Island and ran a chess-checkers stand, playing for quarters. They slept in a bed behind the stand. Grover had an Indian wife, which is to say a Cheyenne or whatever, and the

three of them slept in a bed with Grover in the middle. Arthur insisted there was no hanky-panky, and if he said there were none, then there was none.

"Why? Because Arthur was definitely "one of the boys," and if there were incidents, he would have let me know. His stories about Al Horowitz and himself at the Warsaw 1935 Olympiad were astonishing, and they are probably best left unrelated as interesting as they may be. Arthur always used to say that there was "sex before the Beatles," and based on his testimony, it would appear to be true.

"I asked Arthur what kind of chess player Grover was. He responded that Ken was a lot better at checkers than chess. I pressed him, and he finally said that he was "of course" a master in chess."

Here is Grover's obituary:

Birth: May 10, 1908
Death: Sep. 6, 1993

Kenneth Grover was born in Indiana to Philip and Sophia Grover. From the age of 5 until age 16 he lived in an orphanage and was known for having skipped classes to play checkers.

"The Mighty Mite" played checkers most of his life, holding the 11-Man Ballot World Championship title for several years. He co-authored Twentieth Century Checkers and Let's Play Checkers with his close friend

Introduction by Sam Sloan

Tom Wiswell. He was a master chess player and author of the book "Chess". Playing both checkers and chess Mr. Grover once played 80 opponents simultaneously. He was also known for his blindfold exhibitions.

He was survived by five sons, Charlie, Ron, Tom, Kenneth Grover Jr., all of Taholah and Kenneth Comenout Sr.; five daughters, Jessie Grover Stevens and Annabelle, both of Taholah, Paterica Grover Rains of Onalaska, Lorna Grover of Caracas, Venezuela and Rosalind Lucky of New Jersey; 45 grandchildren and several great-grandchildren.

Married in 1951, he was preceded in death by his wife Tillie Comenout in 1979, three daughters, Phyllis Leahy, Willa Jeanette and Jackie Grover and two brothers.

Services were held at the Coleman Chapel in Hoguiam. Burial: Sunset Memorial Park, Hoquiam, Grays Harbor County, Washington, USA, Find A Grave Memorial# 27968504

Thomas Wiswell wrote the following:

Kenneth Maurice Grover, Sr. died 9/6/1993 at the age of 85, at Taholah, Washington State. He died of kidney failure. Grover was amongst the most respected American crossboard players for several decades. Grover won the World 11 Man Ballot Championship from Newell Banks in 1969, and defended it until losing to Asa Long in 1975. He was also an analyst, author, and exhibition player.

Date: 09-21-1943 Kenneth Grover, formerly of New York, and now with the Seattle-Tacoma Shipbuilding Corporation, issued a challenge to Tacoma's checker players - he would compete against 40 players simultaneously and would even take on 4 of the 40 blindfolded at the U.S.O. club at 415 13th Street. Mr. Grover, author of "Chess" and "Let's Play Checkers" and the US cross board checker champ, opened the competitión to chess aficionados as well. He is pictured (standing, far left) on September 21, 1943, examining the checker moves of Pierce County Sheriff Lee Croft, member of a local checker club. Several other opponents await their turn. Unfortunately, the results of this challenge were apparently not reported in the local newspapers.

Date: 07-19-1943 Description: Workers at the Seattle-Tacoma shipyards came from all walks of life and at least two of them had "checkered" careers. Kenneth (Mighty Mite) Grover, seated left, and Jesse (Bonaparte) Hanson, seated right, would be playing one another Lincoln's birthday, February 12, 1944, for the Pacific Coast Checker Championship. Kenneth Grover, employed at Sea-Tac as an electrician, was a U.S. crossboard checker champion, who played as high as 60 opponents at one time or six blindfolded. A published authority on checkers, he was the runner-up in the previous year's US checker championship. Jesse Hanson, who was a graveyard worker in the labor section at Sea-Tac, was the current Pacific Coast champion and had played in Europe, Mexico, Guatemala and every state in the Union. The three observers are not identified. (Sea-Tac Keel, Vol. III, No. 2, pg. 7; January 19, 1944 issue)

John Donaldson, Captain of the US Chess Team that won the 2016 World Chess Olympiad in Baku, Azerbaijan, writes:

Shuffett)
International Draughts and Checkers (1959 with Marion Tinsley, W. R. Fraser, and Derek Oldbury)
Checkers in Ten Lessons (1959)
Secrets of Checkerboard Strategy, 1960 (reprinted as The Complete Guide to Checkers, 1970)
Art of Checkers (1964, with W. R. Fraser)
Science of Checkers and Draughts (1977)
The Wonderful World of Checkers and Draughts (1980 with Jules Leopold)

Wiswell was also famous for his checkers proverbs. His most famous proverb is "The move that disturbs your position the least disturbs your opponent the most." Another is, "The master knows exactly the right time to do nothing."

Thomas G. Wiswell (Birth: April 25, 1910 - Death: November 14, 1998) Visit Virtual Cemetery

Thomas George Wiswell or Tommy [spelled Tommie in Twentieth Century Checkers and the original printing of Learn Checkers Fast - later Tartan paperback has Tom] was born in NYC on April 25, 1910. {Ken Grover wrote this in a sketch on Wiswell in the first edition of Ryan's Modern Encyclopedia of Checkers, page 175f.} Grover was Wiswell's mentor. Wiswell died November 15, 1998. Al Lyman in ACF Bulletin for February, 1999 at the bottom of p.1. Henry Toder, a long time friend, called Lyman with the information. (Wiswell was 88, judging from his birthdate.) It's too bad that such a fine problemist should have just a two line obit. at the bottom of a page. The next 2001 National GAYP was, appropriately, dedicated to Tom Wiswell.

Introduction by Sam Sloan

His cemetery grave marker at Calverton National Cemetery in eastern Long Island, New York, NY has his death date as Nov 14, 1998 which is most likely the correct date.

Thomas Wiswell of Brooklyn, NY, (The wizard of Gotham). Noted problemist publisher and player has written more books on checkers than any other man with the possible exception of Millard Hopper, and without question he sold more checker books than any other author of the game.

Tom Wiswell's many publications included Let's Play Checkers "LPC" by Tom Wiswell & Kenneth M. Grover (opb) Originally published by David McKay Co, in 1940. This paper-back edition is the eleventh printing, 1972. 188 pages, 5" x 7 ¾", An excellent checker book dealing primarily with the "Cross" and "Double Corner" openings with a good problem section. This was Wiswell's number one all time best seller which covers it all: games, midgames, landings, problems, historical notes. If you can only buy one book - get this one. Learn Checkers Fast "LCF" by Tom Wiswell / Introduction by Jack Dempsey "An invitation to proficiency." published by David McKay, 6th printing, 1946 (pb) 208pgs. Wiswell always has something to teach us, a great classic book. This was Wiswell's number two all time best seller. Both above books as all his book were later published in hard back.

Wiswell won only one major tourney that was the 1938 New York Masters Tourney. However he compiled an excellent record in match play. He won the "go as you please" World Championship from Millard Hopper in 1951 by a score of 7-2-27, and he defended it in

1953 by drawing the match with Hopper 2-2-36. He twice defended the title against Canadian Champion W.R. Fraser winning 2-0-37 in 1956 and by a score of 7-0-27 in 1959-60. Wiswell until his retirement was famous for his cross country exhibition tours. He also appeared on early televisions shows. He was on the game show "What's My Line" and on the Ed Sullivan show.

I probably should not show this game, but it is the only chess game I could find played by Wiswell. It was a simultaneous game played in an exhibition at Lynchburg College in Lynchburg Virginia. I saw an announcement in the newspapers that the World Checkers Champion was giving a simultaneous exhibition. I went to the exhibition but told the exhibitor Thomas Wiswell that I wanted to play him chess, not checkers. With some reluctance, he agreed.

I had brought my chess set to the exhibition so we played on my set as he did not have one. He played about 20 opponents at checkers including several blindfold games and played only me at chess.

I won the game on a blunder. He had a winning position but as he was playing twenty other simultaneous games he overlooked that I could queen a pawn.

```
[Event "Wiswell Simultaneous Checker-Chess Exhibition"]
[Site "Lynchburg, Virginia"]
[Date "1961"]
[White "Wiswell, Thomas"]
[Black "Sloan, Sam"]
[Result "0-1"]
[ECO "B50"]
```

Introduction by Sam Sloan

1.e4 c5 2.Nf3 d6 3.Bc4 Nf6 4.d3 Nc6 5.O-O e6 6.Bg5 a6 7.a3 Qb6 8.Bxf6 gxf6 9.Bb3 Bd7 10.Nc3 Rc8 11.h3 Na5 12.Rb1 Nxb3 13.cxb3 Bh6 14.Nd2 Ke7 15.Nc4 Qa7 16.f4 b5 17.Ne3 b4 18.Na2 c4 19.d4 c3 20.Nxb4 Bb5 21.Rf3 a5 22.Na2 cxb2 23.Rxb2 Rc7 24.Kh2 Rhc8 25.Rff2 Bc6 26.Qd3 a4 27.b4 Qa8 28.d5 Bb7 29.g3 Ba6 30.b5 Bb7 31.Rfc2 Rxc2+ 32.Rxc2 Rxc2+ 33.Qxc2 exd5 34.Nf5+ Kd7 35.Nxh6 dxe4 36.Nb4 e3 37.Nc6 Bxc6 38.Qxc6+ Qxc6 39.bxc6+ Kxc6 40.Nxf7 e2 0-1

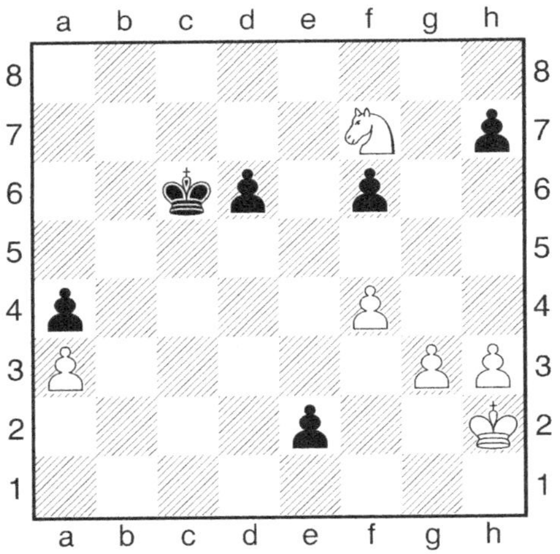

Instead of 40. Nxf7 he had an easy win with either 40. Kg2 or 40. Nf5 catching the pawn.

I was in the 11th Grade in E.C. Glass High School in Lynchburg Virginia. The next day, I went around the school saying "I Beat the World Checkers Champion!"

Introduction by Sam Sloan

Several students at the school expressed disbelief that I had defeated the world's checkers champion. Finally, Bobby Brickhouse sitting two desks away from me in math class, said dryly, "Sam beat him at chess."

When I was hanging around the Flea House also known as the Chess and Checkers Club of New York starting in 1964, Wiswell came there frequently. Usually he was with a group of elderly checkers players and they were analyzing endgames that might come out of the 137 recognized openings. I am sure all of them died long ago.

> "Edgar Allen Poe had a theory that apparently simple and obvious things are very difficult to fathom ....Poe even went so far as to apply this theory of the deceptively obvious to checkers, which he maintained in "The Murders in the Rue Morgue" was a harder game than chess. The very simplicity of checkers, with all the units having similar powers, was, in his opinion, what made the game so difficult. The margin of victory was necessarily small, so that, as Poe put it, "The result" would depend on "some strong exertion of the intellect."

I played checkers as a child. The last time I ever played, the girl next door, Susan Knight, defeated me several games in a row. As I was the Virginia Junior Chess Champion at the time, I could not figure out how a mere girl could beat me at checkers. She won every a game, so it was not a fluke. I remember her father, Sherwood Knight, telling her before the games, "Just do what I told you to do." Ever since, I have been wondering what he told her to do, as that enabled her to win all the games.

After that, I forgot about checkers until the 2011 Mind

Introduction by Sam Sloan

Sports Olympiad in Beijing China. There was a checkers competition going on with the top players from all over the world, alongside with competitions in chess, Chinese chess, go and bridge. I was there as a spectator having just competed in the World Championship of Chinese chess in Jakarta Indonesia and the World Memory Championships in Guangzhou China.

During this competition, Alexander Shvartsman, a former world champion of several varieties of checkers or draughts, was giving a simultaneous exhibition to almost a hundred checkers players, although not all at the same time. I asked him if he could write a book on this, as I am a publisher of books on games, such as go and chess. He said he had a friend working on such a book and would be in contact with me. There were far more players and more interest at the 2011 Mind Sports Olympiad in checkers than in chess, go, bridge or Chinese chess.

Michael Layevskiy, a former Russian now living in the USA, loaned me several books in Russian on draughts, especially books on problems and their solutions. This made me aware that there is a vast literature on the subject, which has largely been ignored.

Most of the recent publicity about checkers has been about competitions to see who was better -- man or machine -- in 1992, 1994 and 1995. Once the game was solved in 2007, there was no need for any more man-machine matches!

What these competitions have established is that the best checkers playing computer, Chinook, is stronger than the best human. The best players can draw the program, since checkers is a draw, assuming perfect play. However, humans are not perfect and eventually they will make a mistake. Even the great Marion Tinsley occasionally erred. This was not absolutely decided because the best human player, Marion Tinsley, who had not lost a game in many years, lost two games to Chinook in 1992, but won the match in part because of computer break-downs. However, in the 1994 rematch, with an improved Chinook, the score was even with six draws when Tinsley withdrew from the match because of illness. The competition did not finish because Tinsley died on April 8, 1995, before the last games could be played, with all of the games being draws.

The programmer of Chinook, Jonathan Schaeffer, has written a book about this, "One Jump Ahead Computer Perfection at Checkers", ISBN 9780387765754

In America, most players play Go As You Please checkers, or GAYP. It has been proven that if the computer has the first move, the computer cannot be beaten, so with best play it is a draw. In order to avoid draws, tournament checkers is played with the drawing of lots or by ballot for the first three moves. Several possible combinations of the first three moves are excluded because they have been believed to lead to forced wins or forced losses. There have been 137 possible combinations of the first three moves allowed in competitive play. Recently several combinations of the first three moves previously believed to be a loss have been shown to be a draw with best play, so they have been added to the list of allowable moves, so there are now 145 combinations allowed for the first three moves.

While Standard American checkers has been thought of an American game, most of the top players nowadays are European. There are now two world championships, the Go As You Please or GAYP champion and the Three-

Move Ballot champion. Recently 3-Move World Champion Michele Borghetti of Livorno, Italy earned right to challenge Sergio Scarpetta for the GAYP World Title in 2016.

There is the question of whether checkers has been solved. www.nature.com/news/2007/070716/full/news070716-13.html A website states that checkers has been solved by computer. One game that has been solved is tic-tac-toe also known as Naughts and crosses. I solved it as a child. A more difficult game is Nim, where a player can take as few or as many items off a heap and whomever is forced to take the last one loses. There is a formula using binary numbers that can be used to solve this game, showing the best move by the player if he has a win and also showing the best defense by the player if he does not have a win. The best defense is one that gives the opponent the best chances to lose.

By this standard, checkers was solved by Jonathan Schaeffer in 2007. Checkers was solved for positions up to 10 pieces. In chess, the positions for up to 7 pieces have been solved. Since checkers has only twelve pieces on each side and there are only two kinds of pieces, it is likely that checkers is truly solved. However, chess will probably never be solved, at least not in this century.

Incidentally, I have some authority on this subject because I was one of the original partners in a computer chess program that eventually became the current computer world chess champion. I was not able to continue in the partnership due to other obligations, but my partner, Don Dailey, did eventually win the Computer World Chess Championship in 2013. Tragically, he died three days before his program Komodo won the world championship.

Introduction by Sam Sloan

I need to thank several checkers players who helped me with this introduction. First is Ed Atkinson, a reformed chess player who reminded me that he twice played me in the Virginia State Chess Championship in 1961 and 1962 when I was a kid. He won both of those games. Next was Bill Salot who directed my questions to The American Checker Federation at http://www.usacheckers.com/forum website where valuable information is available about checkers. Third is George Hay who directed me to websites with biographical information about Kenneth Grover and Thomas Wiswell. A newly typeset edition of Let's Play Checkers is available in PDF format from Bob Newell and his Checker Maven website. The content is the same as this book but the format is somewhat different.

Ed Atkinson writes:

> As a complete beginner at age 13 I bought a copy of Millard Hopper's An Invitation to Checkers. Hopper's stated goal was to take a person with no knowledge of the game to a point where he or she could play a reasonable game against an expert. Nine months later I was regularly drawing one game in every three against Philadelphia Champion, Irwin Altman. Two months later I won a short match for the Bucks County, PA championship.
>
> The match loser lent me a spare copy of Grover and Wiswell's Let's Play Checkers. It was a thrill to go through it, especially Grover's part. I think that it is one of the very best books for the average player ever written. I still refer to it. At the 1968 American Championship I met Ken Grover and we hit it off very well. In round 5 I knew that I would be playing either Grover or Elbert Lowder. I wanted to play Grover but

got Lowder. Two months later at another tournament Grover and I breakfasted together.

Nowadays most checker players rate Wiswell more highly than Grover, probably because he was more in the public eye for a longer time. His go as you please word title was not highly regarded and was thought of as an exhibition title to give publicity to the game and to enhance his career. Grover was the stronger player. He finished third in at least three national tournaments and had impressive match results. After World War Two he gave up being a professional and his results in competition were less impressive In about 1956 Wiswell played on Board Three in a New York versus Pennsylvania Match behind Harold Freyer and Jack Cox. I might be the only living player who knows this.

I intend to try to do further research the life of my friend Kenneth Grover. I think I have established beyond reasonable doubt that Grover really was married to a Native American woman Tillie Comenout who was a Quinault Indian. The name Comenout is associated with Native Americans living in Grays Harbor County, Washington State. It appears that Grover spent the last part of his life living on the Reservation and died there at age 85. Is that the same Indian Woman who lived with him on Coney Island in Brooklyn New York? Did they really have 13 children and what happened to them? These are questions I would like to research.

Sam Sloan
San Francisco, California
USA
October 20, 2016

FOR THE AMERICAN CHECKER CHAMPIONSHIP.

Kenneth M. Grover (right), co-author of LET'S PLAY CHECKERS, is shown matching moves with Asa A. Long World's Champion (left) in the finals of the 10th American Tournament at Flint Michigan

We dedicate this book to
P., R. and M.

K. M. G. and T. W.

FOREWORD

"Let's Play Checkers" is a cordial invitation to participate in a friendly duel of wits. It is a phrase that is used many times daily in all parts of the world. While Checkers is probably the oldest game that man has devised, it is still the most popular of all pastimes, "A hobby of the millions." It is for the ordinary run of players that this book is written. At the same time we believe that the expert, and in fact, all grades of players will find instruction and entertainment in the study of this volume.

In the game section, Mr. Grover has emphasized the best forcing lines for White and Black, thus reducing detail to a minimum. Included in this department are many original lines that Mr. Grover has used with success in his matches, tournaments, and exhibitions throughout the country. In the problem section, which has been prepared by Mr. Wiswell, are one hundred selected positions by America's foremost problem composers. Included are a dozen of Mr. Wiswell's original creations.

There are many other interesting features. They include chapters on the end game and the mid game, a short history of United States checkers, many model three-move games (the expert's style), the latest revised rules for match and tourney play, and other miscellany dealing with various phases of the game.

Some people are inclined to underestimate the game of checkers; they are usually inferior players themselves. Edgar Allan Poe, who was an ardent devotee of the game, once said "Checkers is so simple a game that a child can play it, yet so difficult that no man has been able to master it."

In addition to furnishing relaxation and pleasure, checkers tends to develop many worth while traits and habits, such as patience, good sportsmanship, improvement of the memory, self-control and the ability to concentrate. Therefore—"Let's Play Checkers."

The Authors.

CONTENTS

Introduction by Sam Sloan

"I believe I saw him once at Vancouver 1975 (which Keres won). He may have only visited the tournament. It is likely he married a Native American women as Taholah, Washington, is the headquarters of the Quinault Indians. It is a small, but very beautiful town located on the Pacific ocean in SW Washington. Patent #WAORAA 106646 is a land patent in Grays Harbor, Washington owned by Tillie Comenout. It is a Indian trust patent."

Ownership and use of this patent is overseen by the Bureau of Land Management's Spokane District Office under the serial number WAORAA 106646. The last action for this patent—patent issued—occurred on April 23, 1928. Information on the patent was last updated on July 19, 2011.

Comenout is a Native American name associated with Washington State. **Taholah** is a census-designated place (CDP) on the Quinault Indian Reservation, in Grays Harbor County, Washington State. It seems that Grover was married to Tillie Comenout who was a Quinault Indian.

Now, I am wondering whether she was the same Indian woman he slept with on Coney Island in Brooklyn New York. Also, were the 13 children his children or children from other relationships she had.

I am doing genealogy searches for the name Tillie Comenout on familysearch.org and it comes up with nothing. I cannot find all these Grover children's names either.

Wiswell (London, 1952) stated: 'Kenneth M.

Introduction by Sam Sloan

Grover, when 12 years old, was hailed as a chess child-prodigy, and today he is America's number-one checker player. I wouldn't say "downmarket" for that one. Wiswell was the real world champion for many years, of checkers. I dunno about Grover, but Wiswell was the real thing.

I knew Ken Grover. He was at one point America's Number One Checker Player. He was a chess master too. He won the 1963 Koltanowski Chess Friends Money Tournament in Oakland California, defeating Peter Cleghorn, rated 2350, in the last round.

Last I knew him was in 1967 when he was a professional Poker Player playing every day at the Oaks Club in Emeryville, California.

Grover has almost no published chess games. There is a game in the chess databases where he lost to Grandmaster Isaac Kashdan in Los Angeles in 1954. Here is one of the only games I have been able to find.

```
[Event "Open - AFB"]
[Site "Hamilton AFB, CA"]
[Date "1963.04.28"]
[Round "6"]
[White "Blackstone, John"]
[Black "Grover, Ken"]
[Result "0-1"]
[ECO "C46"]
[PlyCount "84"]
[EventDate "1963.04.28"]
```

1. e4 e5 2. Nf3 Nc6 3. Nc3 Bb4 4. Nd5 Ba5 5. c3 d6 6. h3 Nf6 7. d4 exd4 8. Nxd4 Nxd5 9. exd5 Nxd4 10. Qxd4 O-O 11.

Be2 Bb6 12. Qc4 Qf6 13. O-O Re8 14. Bd2 Bf5 15. Bd3 Re5 16. Be3 Bxd3 17. Qxd3 Bxe3 18. fxe3 Qg5 19. e4 Rae8 20. Rae1 f5 21. Qb5 c6 22. Qxb7 cxd5 23. Qxa7 dxe4 24. Qe3 Qxe3+ 25. Rxe3 g5 26. g3 Kg7 27. c4 d5 28. cxd5 Rxd5 29. b4 Kf6 30. a4 Ke5 31. Ra3 f4 32. a5 Rb5 33. a6 Ra8 34. Ra4 e3 35. a7 Ke4 36. Re1 Kf3 37. gxf4 gxf4 38. Rf1+ Kg3 39. Re1 Kxh3 40. Kf1 Kg3 41. Ke2 f3+ 42. Kf1 Rh5 0-1

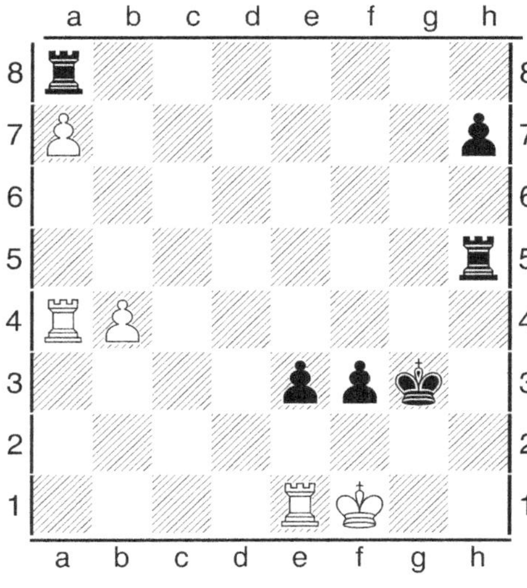

Tom Wiswell (25 APR 1910--14 NOV 1998)

I knew Tom Wiswell too, but not well. He used to come to the Chess and Checker Club of New York at Times Square on W 42nd Street almost every day when I was coming there in 1964 and 1968. There were a bunch of old checkers players there always analyzing endgame positions and sometimes playing too.

Thomas G. Wiswell (April 25, 1910 - November 14, 1998, usually called Tom, sometimes Tommy), from Brooklyn, New York, was a champion checker player, author, and famous problemist (composer of checkers problems). Wiswell was world champion at go-as-you-please checkers (opening moves can be chosen by the players without restriction) from 1951 until he retired in 1975. His world championship matches were 1951 T. Wiswell - M. Hopper 7-2 (with 27 draws), 1953 T. Wiswell - M. Hopper 2-2 (with 36 draws, Wiswell retaining his title), 1956 T. Wiswell - W. R. Fraser 2-0 (with 37 draws), and 1959-60 T. Wiswell - W. R. Fraser 7-0 (with 27 draws). He was famous for his cross-country exhibition tours that he made annually. He also appeared on the Ed Sullivan Show, and What's My Line, and other television shows. Wiswell also served in the U. S. Army, and is buried at Calverton National Cemetery.

Wiswell wrote about 20 more books on checkers (perhaps selling more books than anyone else) including:

Checker Magic (1943)
Learn Checkers Fast (1946, introduction by Jack Dempsey)
Twentieth Century Checkers (1946 with Kenneth Grover)
World Championship Checkers (1950 with Willie Ryan)
Checker Kings In Action (1952 with Millard Hopper)
Checkers Made Easy (1953)
Championship Chess and Checkers for All (1953 with Larry Evans)
Challenge of Checkers and Chess (1955)
America's Best Checkers (1957 with Dr. Robert L.

PRELIMINARY INSTRUCTIONS

As some who read this volume may be studying a checker book for the first time we think the following simple instructions will be appreciated.

The Game of Checkers is played by two people, each moving alternately, one square at a time diagonally, unless he has a jump, in which case he may pass over several of his opponent's men at a time. By studying the Standard Laws and playing over one of the games the newcomer will soon become initiated. For the purpose of recording the play, the squares on the checker board are numbered from one to thirty-two, beginning at the upper left-hand corner and running from left to right as shown on the following diagram.

The Board Numbered

The Men Set for Play

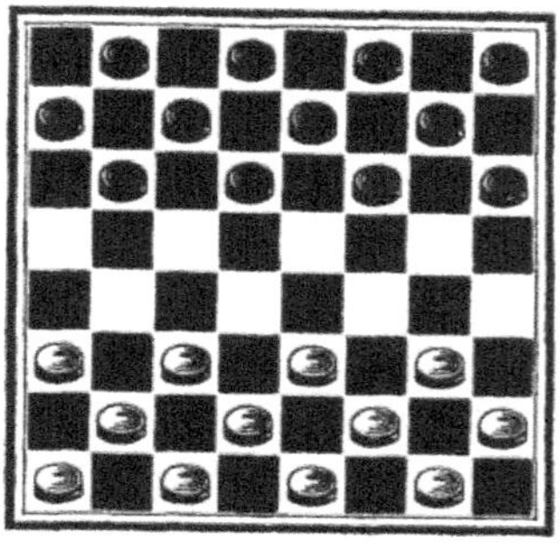

At the start of a game the Black men occupy the squares numbered from one to twelve and the White men occupy the squares from twenty-one to thirty-two. The Black men always move first.

After having numbered your board turn to Game One and see if you can follow the game through to the end. Start with the

first number of the column at the left, which happens to be 11-15. Make this move on your numbered board. Then make the second move which is 23-18, etc. When you reach the bottom of the first row go to the top of the second row and proceed in the same manner. At the end of the fourth column you will find the result of the game which will be Drawn, White Wins or Black Wins.

Some Checker Terms Defined for the Student

Go-As-You-Please, Two Move and Three Move Restriction. These are the three styles employed by the expert in match and tourney play. Under the first named style, which is almost obsolete for serious play, Black may select any opening move he likes. In other words he opens as he pleases. About 1900 the two move restriction became popular and was used in most important matches and tournaments. Under this style of play Black's first move and White's first move is determined by ballot. There are forty-three openings in the official two-move ballot. The reason for introducing two-move restriction was to add scope to the game. The majority of American experts soon had all the two-move openings down so well that there was a popular demand for the introduction of three-move restriction and this style was adopted and used in the 8th American Tournament at Jamestown, New York in 1934. Although it is now used in all important matches and tournaments in America it has not met with much favor with the more conservative English players, although we predict that they will soon follow in the footsteps of their American Cousins in this respect. Incidentally there are 137 playable openings under three-move restriction. This modern style of play calls for Black's first two moves and White's first move to be determined by ballot.

Apex Squares. The Apex Squares are 6, 7 (for Black), 26 and 27 (for White). As a general rule good players consider it inadvisable to move the apex piece in the early part of the game. Of course there are exceptions, the most notable being in the Whilter opening (11-15, 23-19, 9-14, 22-17, 7-11) and the Cross.

Pitch or Sacrifice. When your opponent gives you a man (To get a King or as a tempo move) it is referred to as a Sacrifice or pitch.

The Slip. This maneuver occurs frequently and is best illustrated in the Slip Cross opening: 11-15, 23-18, 8-11, 27-23, and now the Slip comes in via: 11-16, 18-11, 16-20,—causing a simultaneous double exposure of White's pieces on 11 and 24. A rather

fancy play in this particular game but often very practical as well.

Trading Off. This maneuver is also called "Manning Off" or "Swapping Down." This is merely exchanging man for man and is usually employed to advantage by the player who has gained a piece.

Pair-O'-Pants. Also called "Breeches." Here is a simple example of this play. Remove all the pieces from the board. Now put a Black piece on square 14 and a Black King on 16. Place White Kings on squares 22 and 8. With defeat staring him in the face Black is saved by a Pair Of Pants. Black pitches his man on 14 via 14-18, and White must jump 22-15. Black now plays 16-11 (The pants). No matter where White moves Black will jump one of his Kings and draw the game.

THE THEORY OF THE MOVE

While we believe that many authors are inclined to over-emphasize the importance of the move (or opposition) there is no doubt that it is frequently the determining factor in the end-game. It is generally advantageous to have the move but there are times when it is a handicap. Having the move really means having the opposition or last controlling move. Here is a simple illustration:

Black to Play and Win

In the above position Black has the move and wins by playing 18-22. No matter where White moves now Black jumps and thus has the last controlling move.

DECIDING WHO HAS THE MOVE

It is not difficult to determine which side has the move. The first thing we do is literally to divide the board into two vertical systems as shown in the following diagram:

1 2 3 4

29 30 31 32

When playing the Blacks your system would comprise the vertical rows 1, 2, 3, and 4. When playing Whites your system would be made up of the other vertical rows, 29, 30, 31, and 32. Now then, if the opposing forces are equal count all the pieces in your system (Black and White) when it is your turn to play, and if the sum is odd you have the move. If the sum is even then your opponent has the move.

Changing the Move

White to Play

In most cases an exchange will change the move. If you will count the pieces in White's system in the above diagram you will find there are three men in the vertical row 29, none in row 30, one in row 31, and none in row 32. Since the total number of pieces in White's system is even (four) you know that Black has the move. In order to change the move White now makes a trade by playing 26-22, 17-26, 31-22 and Black no longer has the move. For proof, all you need to do is count the number of pieces in Black's system. Since the number is even (2) and it is Black's turn to play we know that White now has the move.

EXCEPTIONS TO THE FOREGOING RULE

Whenever a man becomes blocked in one of the Double Corners (on squares 5 or 28) the move automatically changes. Here is a simple example: Place a Black king on 6 and a man on 12, and White men on 5 and 20. In this position it is Black's turn to play so let's count the number of men in Black's system. Since the total is even (2) we know that White has the move. Black now plays 6-1 and wins because he has the last controlling move though no exchange was made. The student is cautioned to keep this important exception in mind when counting up to find who has the move.

As a rule the move does not change *when both capturing pieces remain on the board.* For example: Place Black kings on 15 and 18 and White kings on 8 and 22. In this position White plays 8-11 and wins despite the fact that an exchange has been made. The point is that after the jumps have been made both the capturing kings are in the same systems as they were before the exchange. *Therefore the move has not been affected.*

It sometimes happens that an exchange is made wherein both capturing pieces remain on the board *but in different systems.* When this occurs the move is changed. For example: Place a Black king on 30 and a man on 11, and a White king on 12 and a man on 22. It is Black's turn to play (note that White has the move) and he moves 30-26. White replies 12-8 and after the jumps have been made Black has the move because in this instance *both capturing pieces are now in different systems.*

GAME SECTION

EDITED BY KENNETH GROVER

The game section has been arranged in such a manner that the two openings most essential to the average player are given the most prominence. You will find that in a large majority of cases, your adversary will start the game with 11-15. In reply it is best that you play 23-18 as it offers the greatest winning chances for White.

When moving first we believe that you will have considerable success with 9-14. This move is very likely to catch your opponent off guard, as few players outside the expert class are really familiar with this opening.

We suggest that you use the following playing guide for openings:

With Whites
(Against 11-15)

Play 23-18
The Cross

With Blacks

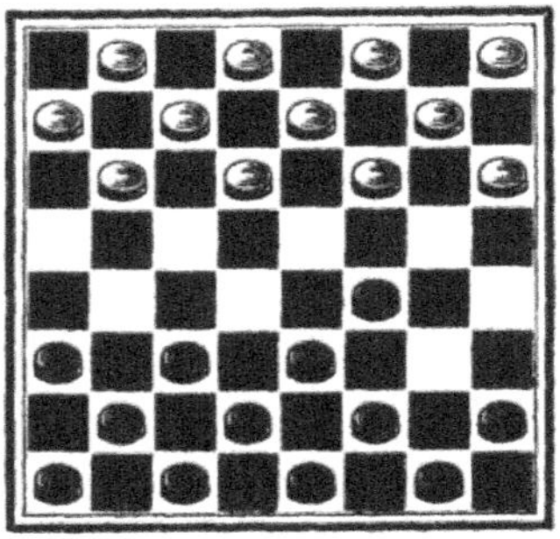

Play 9-14
The Double Corner

Of course you will also have to be prepared to meet the six other opening moves your opponent has at his command (9-13, 9-14, 10-14, 10-15, 11-16, and 12-16) and for that reason the best play on these games has also been included.

Our advice is to make the trunk of Game 1 and Game 13 the

ground work of your study, as they are the master games of the Cross and the Double Corner. Then go over the notes to these games, retaining the ideas involved rather than remembering all the figures like a robot.

Game 1

THE CROSS

11-15—A	18-9	7-11—F	28-19
23-18—B	5-14	22-17	11-15
8-11	22-17—D	2-7—4, 5, G	27-23
27-23	15-18—1, 2	32-27—L	18-27—O
4-8	26-22	1-5—M	31-24
23-19—C	11-15—3, E	24-20—N	15-18—P
9-14	17-13	15-24	19-15
			Drawn

A. This move has proved to be Black's strongest, and has been the usual favorite of the majority of all classes of players from the novice to expert.

B. This move forms the Cross and is favored by many of the Champions in exhibition play. At this stage 23-19 is considered a safer move for a draw but has fewer chances for White to win. The Cross is also more restrictive allowing Black little lee-way in many of the variations. After learning the few weak points of White's game one should be able to score many victories by snaring Black into any one of a number of pitfalls. The average student has been taught to study the 11-15, 23-19 openings, and neglects to study the Cross.

C. The first three moves should be carefully remembered as the whole game depends upon a good start. White is now trying to bind Black's center.

D. With a few exceptions it is more powerful to have the pieces in the center of the board than on the side, as the men in the middle can be moved two ways while the pieces on the side have only the power of moving to one square. In this case, although White relinquishes part of the center, he is cramping and forcing at every turn.

E. Black's path is now straight and narrow. Look what would happen if he tried to go 11-16 instead of 11-15. White would jump

22-15, then 16-23, 31-27, 10-19, 17-10, 7-14, 27-9, 6-13, 24-15; White, having a man to the good plus a strong position, can win handily.

F. Should Black make an attempt to break up the game by 14-17, he would lose a piece as follows: 21-14, 10-26, 19-10. Now in whatever direction Black jumps, White will garner two pieces. For those who find it too troublesome to run over the game each time, may I suggest you play with two boards, one for the main game and the other one to go over the by-plays that are given after some of the moves.

G. The diagram shows the position after White's last move (22-17).

Black to Play

At this stage Black can make three natural moves, which lose, 11-16, 1-5, and 3-7. We shall give an example in the order named:

White wins easily against 11-16 as he can move 31-27, 16-23, 25-22, 18-25, 27-4. Placing the position back to the diagrammed setting, move 1-5, 24-20, 15-24, 28-19, 11-15, 32-28, 15-24, 28-19. White's threat to move 19-15 after Black moves is unavoidable. We again place the position back to the diagrammed setting. 3-7 causes more trouble but the win for White is there. Go 31-27, 6-9—H, J, 13-6, 2-9, 17-13, 1-6, 25-22, 18-25, 29-22, 14-18—K, 30-25, 9-14, 22-17, 11-16, 24-20, 16-23, 25-22, 18-25, 27-2. White wins.

H. 18-23, 27-9, 11-16, 9-5, 16-23, 13-9, 6-22, 25-4. White wins.

J. 1-5, 25-22, 18-25, 29-22, 5-9, 27-23, 15-18, 22-15, 11-27, 32-23, 7-11, 30-26, 11-15, 19-16, 12-19, 23-16, 15-18, 24-19, 18-22, 16-12, 22-31, 12-3, 31-26, 19-15. White wins.

K. 15-18, 22-15, 11-18, 27-23, 18-27, 32-23, 8-11, 24-20, 11-15, 30-26, 15-24, 28-19, 7-11, 19-16. White wins.

L. A trap. This is deceptive as it invites 11-16 on Black's next move.

M. The natural 11-16 favors White because of 27-23, 18-27, and now a subtle move, 13-9, gives White a free king.

N. Up to this point White has not been able to move 24-20 as Black would have pounded the inadequately protected double corner. As Black has now moved 1-5, White has a definite threat viz.: 19-15.

O. White is prepared for the 15-24 jump as then 23-19 is played, paving the way for 19-15 for the two for one.

P. Black can safely give White the opportunity to take the two for two by 19-15 for a quick draw. Now let us imagine Black presses the position and tries to overreach himself and moves 7-11, instead of 15-18, then 30-26, 15-18—Q, 26-22, 11-15 (3-7 gives Black a draw after the two for two by 19-15) and we arrive at this position made famous by Robert Martins.

White to Play and Win

White moves 20-16 and Black is forced to protect the man on 11 and come out 3-7. White pitches a man 13-9, Black jumps 6-13, 24-20, 15-24, 22-6, 13-22, 25-9, 12-19 (Or 5-14), 6-2, 5-14, 2-4. White wins.

Q. If 5-9, 25-22, 14-18, 17-14, 18-25, 14-5, 25-30, 26-23, 30-26, 21-17 (Forcing Black to take the two for one or threatening 17-14 if Black moves the king), 12-16, 19-12, 26-28, 5-1, 15-19, 1-5, 10-15, 5-9, 15-18, 9-2, 18-22, 2-7, 3-10, 12-3 and White wins as played by Peter Doran of Chicago, Ill.

Variation 1

14-18—A	5-9	13-17	11-15
17-14—B	27-23	24-20	23-19
10-17	18-27	10-14	15-24
21-14	32-23	25-22	28-19
7-10—C, D	9-14	17-26	8-11
14-7	22-18	19-16	Drawn
3-10	15-22	12-19	
26-22	25-9	23-7	
1-5	6-13	2-11	
31-27	29-25	30-23	

A. This move admits a narrow draw for Black, giving White a number of chances to win. It is a favorite of non-book players who mistakenly believe it is good.

B. Driving hard to eliminate Black's apex pieces on squares 6 and 7. Unless one receives direct compensation for doing so, it may be disastrous to jump out of these two squares in the opening or early mid-game.

C. 11-16, 19-10, 6-15 can be eliminated by making waiting moves and forcing Black to run out of moves, e.g., 24-20, 16-19, 25-21, 8-11, 29-25, 2-6, 21-17, 18-23, 28-24, 19-28, 26-10, 6-15, 25-21, 15-18, 14-10, 7-14, 17-10, 18-22, and 21-17 toward a king. White wins.

D. 6-10 is the most frequently played move at this stage and after I play 25-21, 10-17, 21-14, 2-6—E, 19-10, 6-15, I gain complete control of Black's double corner and I can win as follows: 14-9 (the man on 9 causes Black to play his pieces from the other side of the board) 12-16, 29-25, 16-19, 25-21, 18-23, 26-22, 11-16, 9-6, 1-10, 22-18, 15-22, 24-6, 7-11, 6-2, 11-15, 31-27, 15-18, 2-6, 22-26, 6-10, 8-12, 10-15 and White wins.

E. 7-10 may make a White win troublesome. Here is how I maneuvered to squeeze a victory when this move was attempted: 14-7, 3-10, 29-25, 11-16—F, 26-22, 16-23, 24-19, 15-24, 28-19, 1-6, 22-15, 10-14, 31-27, 14-18, 19-16, 12-19, 15-10, 6-15, 25-22, 18-25, 27-4, 25-29, 32-27, 2-6, 4-8, 6-10, 8-11, 10-14, 11-16. White wins.

F. If 2-6, 19-16, 12-19, 26-23, 19-26, then White takes three pieces.

Variation 2

6-9	9-13	5-14	12-19
26-23	24-20	30-26	21-17
15-18	11-15	8-11	13-22
17-13	23-18	26-23	25-2
18-27	15-24	11-15	10-15
13-6	18-9	23-18	2-6
2-9	1-5	14-23	23-27
32-23	28-19	19-16	Drawn
			R. Martins

Variation 3

18-23	10-17—D	16-19	19-24
19-15	21-14	24-20	17-13
11-18	6-10—E	7-10	10-14
22-15	14-7	15-6	13-9
10-19	3-19	1-10	11-15
24-15	27-24	25-22	9-6
14-18—A, B	2-7	18-25	15-18
31-27	24-15	29-22	6-2
7-10—C	12-16	8-11	23-27
17-14	28-24	22-17	Drawn
			Drummond

A. Black must beware of many pitfalls in this variation. **7-10** loses by **31-27, 10-19, 17-10, 6-15, 27-4.** White wins.

B. Another trap would be **7-11, 17-10, 11-18, 31-27, 6-15, 25-22, 18-25, 27-4** and White wins.

C. **12-16** walks into a triple by **15-10, 7-14, 17-10, 6-15, 25-22, 18-25, 27-4.**

D. Black can fall into another loss if he jumps **10-19, 14-10, 6-15, 25-22, 18-25, 27-4.** White wins.

E. At the 7th tourney during **1929,** Willie Ryan pitched **23-26, 30-23,** and drew when pitted against Basil Case. They played as follows: **12-16, 14-10** (**28-24** is another draw), **18-22, 25-18, 8-11, 15-8, 6-22, 8-4, 22-26, 29-25, 26-30, 28-24, 30-21, 24-20, 3-7, 20-11, 7-16, 4-8, 21-17, 8-11, 16-20** and after a few moves a draw was called.

Variation 4

6-9	25-22—A	30-25	5-1
13-6	11-15	31-27	26-31
2-9	32-28	22-26	21-17
24-20—A	8-11	6-2	31-26
15-24	29-25	10-15	28-24
28-19	23-26	2-6	12-16
9-13	17-13	25-22	6-2
19-15—A	26-30	17-14	16-19
13-22	13-9	15-19	2-7
15-6	14-18	14-9	19-28
1-10	22-17	19-23	7-16
30-26	18-22	27-18	26-22
3-7	25-18	22-15	Drawn
26-17	15-22	9-5	W. Reid
18-23	9-6	7-10	

A. The key to the game and the only moves needed to be memorized. From this point White has the offensive. Black does not relish 24-20 but is waiting for 17-13 which appears best but is weak and, after 1-6, gives Black a deceptive and powerful attack.

Variation 5

18-23	6-15	13-17	18-22
24-20	25-22—B	22-13	27-18
15-24	18-25	15-18	22-26
28-19	29-22	13-9	30-23
14-18—A	8-11	11-15	19-26
17-14	14-10	9-6	10-7
10-17	2-6	15-19	12-19
21-14	13-9	20-16	Drawn
11-15	6-13	3-8	John
19-10	31-27	6-2	Robertson

A. Black cannot attack the double corner. Should he move 11-15, 19-16, 12-19, 13-9, 6-22, 25-4, White can win.

B. Be careful of 31-27, followed by 25-22 to gain a man, because Black pitches 23-26, 30-23, 15-19, 23-16, 12-19. Now White may be a man ahead but Black's ability to crash through for a free king more than compensates the sacrifice.

Game No. 2

CROSS CHOICE

We present the 36th game between Asa Long and Edwin Hunt in their World's Championship match during 1936.

Edwin Hunt—Black			Asa Long—White
11-15	16-20	2-7	8-11
23-18	24-19	18-15	18-15
9-14—A	8-11	9-13	11-18
18-11	30-26	23-18	28-24
8-15	11-16	14-23	20-27
22-18	29-25	27-18	32-14
14-23—B	10-14	16-23	12-16
27-11	22-18	15-10	14-10
7-16	5-9	7-14	Drawn
25-22	26-22	18-2	
4-8	3-8	23-26	
26-23	31-27	22-18	

A. This move forms the Cross Choice, an even game.

B. 15-22 is more popular because of the natural and easy going style of lines of play involved, plus the possibilities of frequent duplications of positions that occur in other games. (See Mid-Game Structures—A Cross Landing.) In many important encounters this 14-23 jump has been taken. Both sides in this game have a temporary weakness as pieces on 7 and 27 are removed from the board. This move gives greater scope than the 15-22 jump and is favored by many experts, and by those who like to mix the game to get their opponents off the book lanes.

Game 3

11-15, 23-18

11-15	13-22	1-5	11-18
23-18	25-9	17-13	19-15
8-11	5-14	9-14	22-26
27-23	29-25—G	18-9	31-22
4-8	14-18—H, L	5-14	18-25
23-19	26-23	13-9	24-19
10-14—A	18-27	14-18	23-27
19-10	32-23	22-17	20-16
14-23	11-15—N, O	18-23	27-31
26-19	28-24—R	9-6	16-11
7-14—1	2-6—S	15-18	31-27
24-20	21-17	6-2	11-4
6-10—B, C	8-11—W	18-22	27-23
22-17	25-22	2-6	Drawn
9-13—2, 3, F	6-9	3-8	
30-26	23-18	6-15	

A. This line of attack has been prominent in many matches and tournaments and leads toward a variety of play that is of an open character.

B. 14-18, 22-15, 11-18, yields Black's advantage if White accompanies these moves with 32-27, 9-14, 30-26, 5-9, 25-22, 18-25, 29-22, 6-10, 27-23.

C. 11-15 has been tried in opposition, instead of 6-10, but after 19-10, 6-15, the in and out shot by 21-17, 14-21, 30-26, 21-30, 31-27, 30-23, 27-4, puts Black on the defensive. We continue with an example by Jack Cox: 9-14, 4-8, 2-7, 29-25, 5-9, 25-21, 9-13, 32-27, 1-6—D, 27-23, 6-10, 22-18—E, 14-17, 21-14, 10-17, 18-15, 17-22, 23-19, 22-26, 20-16, 26-31, 8-11, 31-27, 11-2, 27-24, 16-11, 13-17, 11-8, 24-20, 15-10, 20-16, 19-15, 16-11. Drawn.

D. G. Clark was defeated by R. J. Allen when he endeavored to draw by: 7-11, 8-15, 14-18, 22-17, 13-22, 21-17, 1-6, 17-13, 3-8, 27-24, 18-23, 15-18. White wins.

E. In many of my exhibitions I have played 8-11, 7-16, 20-11 to bring the game to a climax. Many pushed 10-15 and lost when I cut off 23-19, where instead of 10-15, an easy draw would have been obtained by 12-16, 22-18, 16-19, 18-9, 19-26.

F. This move is the favorite of many players and is considered one of the strongest attacks in the Cross. It is our belief that White now has at least an equal game, with many winning chances, should Black try to force the issue.

G. The accepted defense is 26-23, forcing White upon a narrow tread to hold his draw. I have used 29-25 in many exhibitions and matches, winning or drawing the game every time with ease.

H. 14-18 has the appearance of building up a strong Black attack, but this is more apparent than real. My greatest advantage is that Black may over-play his position, believing that my non-book move is weak. Another reply is 2-7, instead of 14-18. Many players do not realize I have digressed from book play and make the same move they would ordinarily make had I gone 26-23, the book move. Others move 2-7, with the idea I will transpose the game back into the regular channels. Why should White go 26-23, and allow Black to make the powerful 14-17 cut, when 25-22 impels Black to play in careful fashion to sustain a draw? Much has been written about the ability of the expert to transpose an original game into familiar landing fields that arise in many book games. The real test comes when he must resist this opportunity to juggle the position into known lanes, if he feels a better move can be made. Here is an example of the limited mobility of Black's game when 2-7 is made: 2-7, 25-22, 11-15, 26-23—J, 15-24, 28-19, 8-11, 31-26, 11-15, 32-28, 15-24, 28-19, 3-8, 22-17, 8-11, 19-16, 12-19, 23-16, 11-15, 16-12, 14-18, 12-8, 15-19, 17-13, 10-15, 8-3, 18-23, 3-10, 23-30, 20-16, 30-26, 16-12, 26-22—K, 13-9, 15-18, 9-6, 18-23. Drawn—Denvir.

J. Now it is best to accept the chance to transpose the setting into a strong book line for White. Run the trunk game to Note G and move 26-23 instead of 29-25, then 2-7, now 29-25, 11-15 (this is weak, 14-17 is best) 25-22, and we have the same position.

K. D. Hamilton gives a win if 26-31 is played: 12-8, 31-27, 8-3, 27-24, 3-7, 24-28, 13-9, 28-24, 9-6, 1-5, 7-11, 15-18, 11-16, 18-23, 16-20, 24-27, 10-15, 19-24, 15-19. White wins.

L. An easy going game for both sides would be: 11-15, 25-22, 15-24, 28-19, 8-11, 26-23, 11-15, 32-28, 15-24, 28-19, 3-8, 31-26, 8-11, 22-18, 1-5—M, 18-9, 5-14, 19-16, 12-19, 23-7, 2-11, 26-22. Drawn.

M. David Cohen, who is best known for winning a New England tourney which consisted of an array of top-notchers, lost a small stake match to me by making a losing move at this point in the final game, by going: **1-6, 18-9, 6-13, 23-18, 2-6, 18-14, 10-17, 21-14, 13-17, 26-23, 17-22, 23-18, 22-26,** 19-15.

N. Black can take a draw by: **10-14, 25-22, 3-7, 22-18,** 1-5, **18-9, 5-14, 31-26, 7-10, 19-16, 12-19, 23-7, 2-11, 26-22.** Drawn.

O. Interesting play may be evolved from **2-6, 21-17, 6-9** (11-15, 28-24 is trunk), **23-18,** 1-5—**P, 25-21,** 9-14—**Q, 18-9, 5-14, 31-27,** 11-15, **27-24,** 8-11, 17-13, 14-18, 13-9, **18-23, 9-6, 23-27, 6-2, 27-31** 2-7. White wins.

P. 9-13 loses by **25-22,** 1-5, **31-27, 3-7, 27-24.** White wins.

Q. At this point 9-13, **17-14,** shows promise for White to win and I leave it for the critics and analysts to decide.

R. A tricky move and a pet variation of mine.

S. If 8-11, 21-17, 1-5, 25-22, 5-9, **23-18—T, 10-14—U, V, 17-10, 2-7, 10-6, 9-13, 19-10, 7-23, 22-18.** White best.

T. A danger point for White is **17-13, 2-6, 23-18, 12-16, 19-12,** 10-14 causing White trouble. This is the main defensive key position to remember. If you will watch out for this one trap, as it may be transposed from some of the other lines of play, you should have clear sailing, with Black having the laboring oar.

U. The pitch by **11-16, 20-11, 3-7** draws by **17-13, 7-23, 13-6, 2-9, 18-11.** Drawn.

V. 9-13 loses by **31-27, 11-16** (If 2-6, 18-14), **20-11,** 3-7, 11-8, 7-11, **27-23, 11-16, 18-11,** 16-20, **23-18,** 20-27, **18-14.** White wins.

W. **6-9, 25-22, 9-14—X, Y,** (If 8-11, 23-18. If 1-5, 23-18) **17-13,** 1-5—Z, **20-16, 3-7, 16-11, 7-16, 24-20, 15-24, 20-4, 14-17, 22-18, 10-14, 18-9, 5-14.** Drawn.

X. **1-6, 20-16, 3-7, 23-18, 8-11, 31-27.** White wins.

Y. **9-13, 23-18, 8-11, 31-27, 10-14** (If 1-5, 18-14), **17-10, 13-17, 22-13, 15-22, 27-23, 22-26, 23-18, 26-31, 19-15, 3-8, 24-19, 1-5, 10-7, 31-27, 7-3, 27-23, 18-14.** White wins.

Z. **1-6, 20-16, 3-7, 16-11, 7-16, 24-20, 15-24, 20-4, 10-15, 4-8, 15-19, 23-16, 12-19, 8-11, 24-28, 11-16, 19-24** (If 19-23, then 22-18, 14-17, 16-19, 23-26, 31-22, 17-26, 18-14, and the man on 6 is snared in a few moves) **16-19, 14-17, 19-15, 17-26, 31-22, 28-32, 22-17, 32-27, 15-19, 24-28, 17-14, 28-32, 19-15, 27-23, 14-9.** White wins.

Variation 1

The 6-15 jump was popular with many of the Scottish players at the beginning of the century, but it has been neglected of late.

6-15	22-18	6-9	14-10
19-10	16-20	15-10	23-26
7-14	17-14	9-13	11-16
24-19	9-13	10-6	26-31
11-16	30-26	17-22	21-17
19-15—A	2-7	26-17	31-26
16-19	32-27	13-22	18-14
22-17	1-6	6-2	26-23
14-18	27-24	8-11	17-13
25-22	20-27	20-16	3-8
18-25	31-24	11-20	16-12
29-22	13-17	2-11	8-11
12-16	24-20	19-23	Drawn

Stewart vs. R. Jordan

A. Those desiring simplification may play 22-17, 16-23 17-10, 2-7, 31-26, 7-14, 26-19, 8-11, etc. Draws.

Variation 2

14-18	18-27	26-31	17-14
32-27	31-24	18-15	4-8
9-14	14-18	31-26	14-18
30-26	17-14	29-25	15-10
5-9	10-17	26-30—B	6-15
26-22	21-5	20-16—C	19-10
2-6—A	18-23	30-21	12-16—D
22-15	25-22	16-11	8-11
11-18	23-26	21-17	16-20
27-23	22-18	11-4	24-19

And continue: 20-24, 19-16, 24-27, 16-12, 27-31, 11-7, 18-22, 28-24, 31-27, 24-20, 27-23, 20-16, 22-18, 7-2, 18-14, 2-7, 14-18, 7-11, 18-14, 11-7. Drawn by perpetual check.

A. This line favors White and hasn't been used much in serious encounters. Black starts on the down grade if 18-23, 27-18, 14-23, 22-18.

B. A safer draw is 26-31, 15-10, 6-15, 19-10, 8-11, 25-22, 31-27, 22-18, 27-23, 18-15, 11-18, 10-6, 1-10, 20-16, 12-19, 24-6.

C. Improves 25-21 and was suggested by Denvir.

D. This move is where Denvir leaves us.

Variation 3

11-15	3-7—4, A	7-10—D	26-31
17-13	20-16—B	16-11	6-13
15-24	9-13	6-9	31-27
13-6	30-26	25-21	18-9
2-9	1-6	10-14	5-14
28-19	29-25	22-18	13-17
8-11	14-17—C	13-17	27-18
25-22	21-14	11-7	17-10
11-15	10-17	17-22	18-15
32-28	26-23	7-2	Drawn
15-24	17-26	22-26	
28-19	31-22	2-6	

A. Newell Banks, World's Blindfold Champion, defeated George Wareham on this variation: 9-13, 30-26, 5-9, 31-27, 3-7, 20-16, 1-5, 29-25, 14-17, 21-14, 10-17, 25-21, 9-14, 27-23. White wins.

B. Made to prevent 7-11, followed by 11-15.

C. The win on 6-9 transposes into Note A and is 31-27, 14-17, 21-14, 10-17, 25-21, 9-14, 27-23, 5-9, 22-18, 7-10, 18-15, 17-22, 26-17. White wins.

D. Another draw line would be: 6-9, 25-21, 9-14, 22-18, 13-17, 18-9, 5-14, 23-18, 14-23, 21-14, 23-26, 14-9, 26-31, 9-6, 31-27, 19-15, 12-19, 6-2. Drawn—Hanson vs. Reynolds.

Variation 4

3-8—A	7-2	13-29	11-7
20-16	12-16	19-16—C	22-18
9-13	2-7	27-31	16-11
30-26	16-20	26-23—C	5-9
5-9	27-23	31-27	12-8
29-25	19-24	23-19—D	9-13
1-5	23-19—B	29-25—E	7-2
31-27	24-27	16-12	20-24
10-15	7-10	27-24	8-3—G
19-10	14-18	19-16	
12-19	22-15	25-22	
10-7	9-14	15-11	
8-12	10-17	24-19	

A. Appears stronger than the usual 3-7. My opponent at this sitting was Walter Alexander, fifteen year old boy wonder of the Bronx whom I have taken under my wing. I predict he will make a name "Checkeristically" in the near future.

B. The usual procedure is the way M. Barrie and J. Currie played it and is safer for White, continuing: 22-18, 24-27, 25-22, 27-31, 7-10, 20-24, 10-17, 31-27, 17-14, 24-28, 14-10, 28-32, 10-14, 32-28, 14-17, 28-32. Drawn by perpetual check.

C. Preparing to line up three men (on squares 15, 16, and 26) to the king row.

D. The correct method in lining up three pieces when attacked by a king. It should be mentioned that when two pieces are running the gauntlet, they should be separated in going for a king.

E. 27-23, 15-10, 29-25, 19-15, 23-19, 16-12—F, 25-22, 15-11, 22-18, 10-7. Draw.

F. 16-11 would lose by 25-22, 11-8, 19-16, forcing the man on square 15 to be trapped on the next move.

G. The three pieces have made a safe passage through the blockade.

Game 4

SLIP CROSS

11-15	25-22	2-6—M	13-6
23-18	8-11	30-26	15-19
8-11	29-25—D	6-9	24-15
27-23	10-15—E, F, G	14-10	3-7
11-16—A	18-14	9-14	10-3
18-11	9-18	26-23	1-26
16-20	23-14	5-9	3-7
31-27—B	6-9—H, L	22-17	26-30—O
7-16	26-23	15-18—N	
22-18—C	9-18	17-13	
4-8	23-14	11-15	

A. Styled the Slip Cross.

B. 24-19 is the accepted move giving Black many chances to trap White. The text is an old line of play but is rarely adopted by the experts. We have obtained many clean cut and decisive wins with 31-27.

C. Commanding the center.

D. 24-19 is being held back to prevent running the game into the line of play that arises from note B.

E. Of course if 10-14, White gets a quick king by 21-17, 14-21, 18-14, 9-18, 22-8. White wins.

F. Against 9-14, 18-9, 5-14, 22-18 was published to win by J. Robertson, but instead of 22-18, 22-17 is the preference of the Detroit Chess and Checker Club members to win. The play: 22-17, 3-8 (baiting a trap that turns into a boomerang), 25-22, 10-15, 17-10, 15-19, 24-15, 11-25, 28-24, 6-15, 23-19, 16-23, 27-4 and White wins.

G. 3-8 is untenable after 18-15, 10-19, 24-15, 11-18, 22-15. White wins—E. Clark.

H. Play on 3-7 was published to draw by Clark, as follows: 26-23, 16-19—J, 23-16, 12-19, 22-18, 15-29, 24-8, 29-25, 30-26, 6-10, 8-3, 10-17, 21-14, 2-6, 3-10, 6-15, 14-10, 25-21, 10-7, 21-17, 7-3, 15-18, 27-24. Drawn.

J. 6-10, 30-26, 10-17, 21-14, 1-6, 25-21, 6-10, 23-18, 10-17, 21-14, 2-6—K, 27-23, 20-27, 14-10, 7-14, 18-2, 15-19, 2-7, 27-31, 7-3, 11-15, 23-18, 5-9, 18-11, 19-24, 28-19, 16-30, 22-17. Drawn—E. Clark.

K. 16-19, 22-17, 15-31, 24-8, 31-24, 28-19, 7-10, 14-7, 2-11 and White is best—E. Clark.

L. 16-19 loses by 27-23, 20-27, 23-7, 3-17, 32-23. White wins.

M. If 16-19, 21-17, 11-16, 25-21, 2-6, 14-10, 5-9, 17-13, 9-14, 22-17, 14-18, 17-14, 18-22, 14-9. White wins.

N. 9-13, 25-22, 3-8 (14-18, 23-14, 3-8, Black draws), 23-19, 16-23, and 27-9, 20-27, 32-23. White wins.

O. Published play by E. Clark ends here. The ending is continued with 7-10, 14-17, 21-14, 30-21, 14-9, 18-22, 10-15, 21-25, 9-6, 22-26, 6-2, 25-22, 2-7, 26-31, 15-18, 22-15, 7-2, 31-24, 28-10, 16-19, 2-7, 20-24, 7-11, 19-23. Drawn.

Game 5

11-15, 23-18

11-15	6-10—B, C	5-9	11-15
23-18	25-21	26-17	20-11
8-11	10-17	9-14	15-24
27-23	21-14	31-26—H	23-19
9-13—A	2-6	14-21	24-27
18-14	32-28	26-22—J	11-7
10-17	7-10—D, E	10-15	27-31
21-14	14-7	22-17	7-2
4-8	3-10	6-9	31-26
23-18	26-23—F	13-6	2-6
12-16	13-17	1-10	26-22
24-20	22-13	24-19	Drawn
8-12	15-22	15-24	
28-24	30-26—G	28-19	

A. White has most of the choice in routing what channels shall be pursued in this variation.

B. Years ago one tried 6-9 against the mighty Richard Jordan and fell down to defeat in the following manner: 32-28, 2-6, 22-17, 13-22, 26-17, 15-22, 25-18, 6-10, 18-15, 9-18, 15-8, 7-11, 8-4, 3-8, 30-26, 1-6, 29-25, 5-9, 17-14, 10-17, 26-22, 17-26, 31-15, 11-18, 4-11. White wins.

C. A danger point for Black is moving 16-19. This is a losing move that often traps the inexperienced player. The win: 32-28, 6-9 (if 6-10, 22-17), 14-10, 7-23, 22-18, 15-22, 24-8, 23-27, 26-17 (the man on 22 is snared), 13-22, 31-24. White wins.

D. Let us look at the diagram:

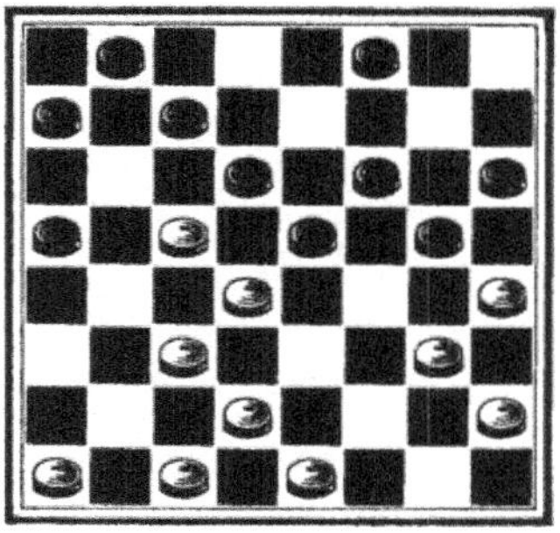

Those who have followed checkers for any length of time must realize that some theories are good and many "not so good." One theory that has been espoused is that it is dangerous to break up your king row. For the amateur I will add that he might find it safer keeping his king row intact, but if he sees an idea (whether it be book or not) that calls for such tactics, then let him break his king row.

This innovation, which breaks up Black's king row and plays havoc with an apex piece, looms as unorthodox and against many of the general principles which we take for granted. There are a multitude of maneuvers similar to this one that never reach the books until they are first tested by the analysts and experts to make sure they are sound.

The fallacy in the minds of the public is that the expert knows every possible move. If this were true, the game would be mastered and would naturally lose its appeal, offering no new roads for exploration. Even after a move has been accepted, new play is sometimes uncovered that makes the line untenable—and another book game must be discarded.

E. The regular book moves given are taken from a game between Messrs. Swan and Adamson. Continuing: 6-10, 29-25, 10-17, 25-21, 1-6, 21-14, 6-10, 30-25, 10-17, 25-21, 7-10, 21-7, 3-10, 18-14, 10-17, 26-23, 17-26, 31-22, 5-9, 24-19, 15-24, 28-19, 9-14, 22-18, 14-17, 19-15, 17-22, 15-8, 16-19. Drawn.

F. 24-19 loses by 15-24, 28-19, 16-23, 26-19, 6-9 (5-9 permits a draw by 19-15, 10-19, 29-25, 6-10, 18-14), 29-25, 9-14, 18-9, 5-14, 31-27, 11-15, 27-24, 14-18. Black wins—deBearn.

G. deBearn's draw is by 30-25, 5-9, 25-18, 10-15, 24-19, 15-22, 19-15, 11-27, 31-24, etc.

H. 23-18 barely draws by 14-23, 29-25, 1-5, 25-22, 23-27, 22-18, 10-15, 18-14, 15-18, 24-19, 16-23, 31-24, 23-26, 24-19, 18-23, 20-16, 11-20, 19-15, 26-30, 14-10. Drawn.

J. Watch out for 23-18. In a practice game I lost believing I could win on a long ending by 10-15, 18-14, 15-18, 14-9, 6-10, 9-6, 18-23, 26-19, 16-23, 6-2, 23-27, 24-19 and in my mind the win was there in a few more moves. Now, placing the position back to note J, my opponent—who was Mr. L. T. deBearn, my former coach, and my host when I performed at the Detroit Chess and Checker Club during December, 1939, was silently waiting for this combination. After going 23-18, he gently pushed 6-9!, 13-6, 10-15. "It's all over." It was a case of seeing twenty moves ahead and not two.

Game 6

11-15, 23-18

11-15	15-24	11-15	7-11
23-18	28-19	31-26	6-2
8-11	4-8	15-24	11-15—D
27-23	29-25	22-18	2-7
10-14	8-11	6-9	15-24
22-17—A	25-22	13-6	28-19
15-22	7-10	24-27	26-23
17-10	17-13	18-9	22-18
6-15	9-14	5-14	23-16
25-18—A	30-26	23-19	18-9
15-22	3-7—B	27-31	10-15
26-17	22-17	26-22	9-6
11-15	2-6	31-26	Drawn
24-19	26-22	32-28—C	

A. Louis Ginsberg adopted this line in his match with Sam Gonotsky. Mr. Ginsberg adopted many lines that offered opportunities to switch from the book play forcing his opponents to create new developments. In choosing lines of play for tournaments or matches, I have tried to use these same tactics on some of the openings. In a weak game I plan lines that can't be varied so easily, but if I have the strong side I complicate the game to give my opponent all the chances he wants to mix things. Certain openings are my favorites such as the Double Corner and the Cross. I have memorized these and other lines to use as my groundwork and rarely swerve into unknown paths.

B. The Gonotsky-Ginsberg game was played in the following manner:

11-15	7-11	15-19	19-26
32-27	18-9	23-16	31-22
15-24	5-14	12-19	14-18
27-20	13-9	6-2	22-17
2-7	11-15	10-15	Drawn
22-18	9-6	26-23	

C. Watch out for 19-15, 10-19, 17-3, 26-17, 21-14, 1-17. Black wins.

D. White wins if 26-30, 2-6, 11-15, 6-9, 15-24, 28-19.

Game 7

11-15, 23-18

11-15	26-23	13-22	24-20
23-18	6-9—B, C	25-9	15-24
8-11	30-26	1-5	28-19
27-23	9-14—E	29-25	11-15
4-8	18-9	5-14	20-16—H
23-19	5-14	25-22	15-24
9-13—A	22-17—F, G	2-6	22-18

And continue: 12-19, 18-2, 8-11, 23-16, 11-20, 2-11. White wins—F. Wendemuth.

A. This losing move forms diagrammed position. The loss was first published in 1756 by William Payne.

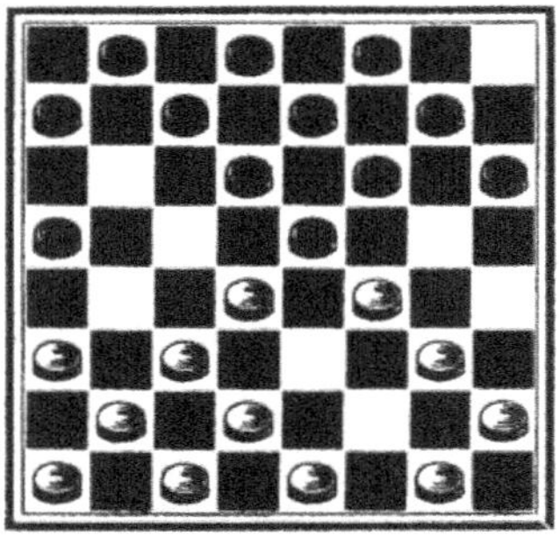

White to Play and Win

B. Black is making an attempt to loosen the cramp that is binding his whole center. If 10-14 is played White would win by 18-9, 5-14, 19-10, 6-15, 22-18, 15-22, 25-9, 1-5, 29-25, 5-14, 25-22, 2-6, 22-18, 6-9, 24-20, 7-10, 28-24, 12-16, 24-19, 8-12, 30-25, 13-17, 25-22, 17-26, 31-22, 3-8, 32-28.

C. Let us assume your opponent had moved from 5-9, then 21-17, 10-14—D, 17-10, 7-14, 19-10, 6-15, 25-21, 2-7, 24-19, 15-24, 28-19, 7-10, 31-27, 11-16, 18-15, 1-6, 29-25, 16-20, 30-26, 3-7, 22-18, 7-11, 25-22, 11-16, 32-28 and White wins—T. Cowie.

D. In a simultaneous exhibition at Orillia, Ont., Canada, my opponent tried a gambit to release the cramp by 12-16, 19-12, 15-19.

(1-5 would be annihilated several ways, one of which is by 24-20, 9-14, 18-9, 5-21, 23-18, 15-19, 31-26. White wins.) Continuing after 15-19, jump 24-15, 10-26, 30-23, 7-10, 32-27, 9-14, 18-9, 1-5, 25-21, 5-14, 27-24, 11-15, 24-20, 2-7, 23-19, 15-24, 28-19, 14-18, 22-15, 13-22, 20-16, 10-14, 31-27, 14-18, 27-24, 6-9, 21-17, 9-13, 17-14, 22-26, 15-11, 8-15, 19-10, 26-31, 24-19, 31-27, 19-15, 27-24, 15-11. White wins.

E. It will be noticed that 2-6 loses easily by 19-16, but 10-14 instead may cause a little trouble. To effect the win, jump 19-10, then 2-6, 24-19, 6-24, 28-19, 11-16, 22-17, 13-22, 26-10, 7-14, 25-22, 9-13, 18-9, 5-14, 29-25, 1-5, 22-18, 13-17, 18-9, 5-14, 25-22. White wins—Published Play.

F. Our reason for going 22-17 at this stage, and not 22-18, is that the former holds the cramp on Black, whereas 22-18 permits the release of the strangle hold. Notice that after 22-18, 15-22, 25-9, 1-5, Black, with the removal of the piece on 15, will be able to develop the men now located in the single corner and middle of the board.

G. The books also give 32-27 to win but this is more forceful.

H. A tempo that cinches the game.

Game 8

11-15, 23-18, 9-13

11-15	28-24	2-7	12-8
23-18	4-8	32-28	11-16
9-13—A	24-20	11-15	8-3
18-11	5-9	28-19	16-20
8-15	21-17	15-24	3-7
22-17	15-19	20-16	24-27
13-22	17-13	12-19	20-27
25-11	8-11	23-16	31-24
7-16—B	29-25	14-17	26-22—D
24-20	9-14	21-14	Drawn
3-8—C	25-21	10-17	
20-11	19-24	16-12	
8-15	27-23	7-11	

A. Black has a difficult task in handling his side of the game, and the wins for White are numerous.

B. White's strength is based on the weakness of Black's disorganized single corner.

C. Denvir drew against Bradford with the following: 16-19, 29-25, 10-15, 25-22, 6-10, 22-17, 5-9, 17-13, 1-6, 27-24, 9-14, 26-22, 3-7, 22-17, 4-8, 32-27, 8-11, 30-26, 14-18, 17-14, 10-17, 21-14, 6-10, 13-9, 10-17, 9-6, 2-9, 26-23, 19-26, 31-6, 12-16, 6-2, 16-19, 27-23, 19-26, 24-19, 15-24, 28-19, 18-23, 19-16, 26-31, 16-12, 31-26, 12-8, 26-22, 8-3. Drawn.

D. Ryan and Dell drew this well played game in the Ninth Tourney.

Game 9

11-15, 23-18, 10-14

11-15	21-14	23-27—L	31-24
23-18	9-25	32-23	20-27
10-14—A	29-22	7-11	6-2
18-11	5-9	23-18	10-15
8-15	27-23	16-23	13-9
26-23—B	9-14	18-14	11-16
6-10	23-18—E	11-16	9-5
22-17—C	14-23	14-7	27-31
1-6	22-17	2-11	5-1
23-19—C	12-16	17-14	15-19
4-8	19-12	16-20	1-6
25-22	11-16—F	14-9	16-20
8-11	24-19	6-10	30-25
17-13	15-24	9-6	Drawn
14-17—1, D	28-19	23-27	

A. Favors White but the opening has winning chances for either side. The above is a game played between Harold Freyer and myself in the 1939 Washington Birthday Tournament, held in New York City when we split first and second prizes.

B. Best. 24-19 and 24-20 are secondary choices and lack force. This opening can arise from 10-14, 22-18, 11-15, 18-11, 8-15, 26-22.

C. Cramping both the single and double corners.

D. A matter of choice which is best—14-17, or 14-18 as taken by me. See Variation 1.

E. 31-26 is the book move and leads to a strong ending for White. I have a penchant for pitching pieces in mid-games to secure positional advantage. This type of strategy has won many games for me, but penalties have likewise accrued for my daring. In the 9th tourney during my heat with Ray Gould, many times New England champion, with a draw in sight, I went down a man believing I had a beautiful draw many moves away. Ray Gould aptly placed the comment in the 9th tourney book "The piece is lost, never to be regained."

In the $1000 stake match between Sam Gonotsky and Mike Lieber, the following hard draw for Black ensued:

31-26	7-11	13-6	10-15
14-17	22-18	2-9	7-16
24-20	3-7	16-12	15-19
15-24	19-16	10-14	16-11
28-19	12-19	12-8	19-24
11-15	23-16	14-23	11-15
32-28	17-21	8-3	23-27
15-24	26-22	7-10	15-18
28-19	6-9	3-7	9-13
			Drawn

F. 15-18 complicates matters and both sides have to be careful. For instance: 31-27 (only move), 11-15—G, 24-20 (only move), 7-11—H, 30-25 (only move), 23-26, 20-16, 11-20, 27-24, 20-27, 32-7. Drawn. All the other variations favor White.

G. 11-16, 24-20, 7-11 (16-19 is Note H), 28-24, 10-15, 17-14, 6-10, 14-7, 3-10, 12-8, 16-19, 8-3, 19-28, 3-7—J, 10-14—K, 7-16, 23-26, 30-23, 15-19. Drawn.

H. 15-19, 30-25 (the key to the situation), 7-11, 25-21, 11-15, 17-14, 10-17, 21-14, 6-10, 14-7, 3-10, 27-24, 23-26, 12-8, 10-14, 8-3, 19-23, 3-8, 23-27. Drawn.

J. 27-24, 10-14, 3-7, 18-22, 7-16, 15-18. Drawn.

K. White wins if 15-19 is played. After the jump 7-14, 19-24, 14-10, 24-31, 10-15 White can win the ending.

L. A nice pitch which clears up Black's position at once.

Variation 1

In the other side of the opening, Freyer and I continued with this game:

14-18	31-26	20-24	13-6
21-17	10-19	23-18	11-18
18-25	27-23	24-27	6-2
30-21	18-27	19-15	14-10
3-8	32-7	27-31	2-6
29-25	2-11	17-14	10-7
15-18	28-24—A	31-26	21-17
19-15	12-16	14-10	18-23
10-19	26-23	26-23	17-14
24-15	16-20	10-1	7-11
7-10	24-19	23-14	Drawn

A. 26-23 is preferred and was the move taken by Mike Lieber when he was paired with R. T. Ward in the 1927 International match.

Game 10

11-15, 23-18, 7-11

11-15	24-15	6-9	26-23
23-18	10-19	27-24	13-22—B
7-11—A	23-16	11-15	23-14
27-23	12-19	18-11	22-26
3-7	22-17	8-15	30-16
32-27	9-13	21-17	7-10
15-19	17-14	9-18	Drawn
			H. F. Shearer

A. This game slightly favors White.

B. The alternate 18-27, draws by 24-20, 13-22, 25-11, 7-16, 31-15, 16-19, 20-16, 5-9, 29-25, 9-14, 15-10, 14-18, 25-22, 18-25, 30-21, 19-23, 28-24, 23-27, 24-20, 27-31, 10-7. Drawn.

Game 11

11-15, 23-18, 15-19

Charles W. Tupper—Black Willie Ryan—White

11-15	24-20—B	9-13	5-9
23-18	5-9	29-25—D	2-7
15-19	20-11	3-7—E	21-17
24-15	19-23	14-9	11-16
10-19	26-19	7-16	9-6
22-17	15-24	31-27	16-20
12-16	28-19	6-10	27-24
17-14	6-24	9-5	20-27
7-11	25-22	4-8	32-16
27-24	24-28	5-1	15-19
11-15	30-26	8-11	22-15
18-11	1-6—C	1-5	13-29
8-15	22-17—D	10-15	15-11—F
14-10	14-18	26-22	Drawn
9-14—A	17-14	16-19	

A. 4-8, 25-22, 9-14, 22-18, 14-23, 24-20, 8-11, 10-7, 3-10, 28-24, 19-28, 26-12, as played between Stephen Fairchild and Kenneth Grover is very weak if not a loss for Black.

B. Playing it safe. White can play 25-22, 5-9, 22-17*, 4-8, 24-20 (17-13, 16-20), 8-11, 32-27 (17-13, 14-18), 9-13*, 30-25 (27-24, 13-22, 26-17, 6-9), 13-22, 25-9, 6-13, 29-25, 2-7. Drawn—W. Ryan.

C. Anything else here would give White a very powerful game. If 3-7, then 22-17; if 3-8 then 26-23, 8-15, 31-27 etc.; if 1-5, 22-17, 14-18, 17-13, etc.—W. Ryan.

D. The right combination to draw.—W. Ryan.

E. 3-8, 11-7, 2-11, 31-27, 13-17, 14-10, 6-15, 21-14, 8-12, 14-9, 4-8, 9-6, 11-16, 26-23 also draws.—W. Ryan.

F. This game and notes was kindly submitted by Harold Freyer.

Game 12

11-15, 23-18, 12-16

11-15	15-22	8-11	8-12
23-18	25-9	25-22	24-19
12-16—A	5-14	2-6	11-15
18-11	28-24	26-23	19-16
8-15	4-8—D	6-9	12-19
24-20—B	24-19	30-26	23-16
9-14—C	16-23	3-8	15-19
20-11	27-9	32-28	16-11
7-16	6-13	1-5	19-23
22-18	29-25	28-24	26-19
			Drawn

A. Black now has a hard draw.

B. White makes an immediate attack on the single corner planning to dislodge the piece on 7.

C. Black might try going 7-11, but after 26-23 the position is considered untenable, because of the cramping of the single corner pieces.

D. Arthur Reisman played 16-20 against me in the 9th tourney and lost, missing a hard analytical draw. The game: 24-19, 4-8, 29-25, 8-12—E, 25-22, 3-8, 32-28, 2-7, 26-23, 6-9, 22-18, 8-11, 18-15, 11-18, 21-17, 14-21, 23-5, 10-14, 19-15, 14-18, 31-26, 12-16, 15-11, 7-10, 11-7, 16-19, 7-2, 10-14, 2-7, 1-6, 7-11, 6-9, 11-15. White wins.

E. 6-9 is the move claimed by the analysts to hold a draw.

Game 13

9-14, 22-18, 5-9, 24-19

9-14—A	7-11	14-17	11-27
22-18	25-22—1, D	21-14	18-2
5-9	1-5—E	10-17	27-32
24-19	27-24—F, G	19-16—P, Q	2-6
11-15	16-20	12-19	32-27
18-11	32-28—K, L	23-16	6-10
8-24	20-27	17-22	27-23
28-19	31-24	26-17	10-14
4-8	9-13	13-22	22-26
25-22	18-9	28-24—R, S	30-25
8-11	5-14	6-10	26-30
22-18—B	24-20—M	16-12	25-21
11-16	2-7	10-15	Drawn
29-25—C	22-18-N	20-16—T	

A. The commencement of the Double Corner and a good alternative for the favorite 11-15. The Double Corner with the Black side, and the Cross when my opponent starts off with 11-15 has been used successfully in all my exhibition tours. Seventy-five years ago the opening was held doubtful but is now the preference of many headliners.

B. Moves like 23-18 are futile as the exchange causes an unfortified double corner leaving the squares 27 and 23 vacated without any advantage for the maneuver. To make a cut like 23-18, some direct aim must first be had.

C. Players sometimes try 18-15 to dash for the king row but 3-8, 29-25 and 1-5 is made with the idea of smashing White's center. White moves 26-22, 14-18, 23-14, 16-23, 27-18, and jumps the single man 10-19, leaving White with a cramped single corner and no double corner. The common finish is 30-26, 8-11, 31-27, 11-16, 27-23, 16-20, 23-16, 12-19, 21-17, 9-13, 25-21, 20-24. Black wins.

D. If 26-22 is made, the cut by 10-15, 19-10, 6-15, can be made with success. Black has a definite object in cutting up the middle, even at the expense of taking away the piece on square 6. White cannot move a piece on the single corner side and the only playable piece on the other side is from 27-24 (as 31-26 is beaten immediately by 16-20, 32-28, 15-19). The pieces on 9, 11, 14, 15, and 16 are completely cramping all of White's forces. Continuing the play after 27-24, 16-20, 32-28, 20-27, 31-24, 2-7, 24-19, 15-24, 28-19, 7-10, 30-26, 3-7 and White can resign.

E. This position can arise from the Cross opening, colors reversed, viz.: 11-15, 23-18, 8-11, 27-23, 4-8, 23-19, 9-14, 18-9, 5-14. 22-17, 15-18, 32-27 (about the equal of 26-22 that we offered in Game 1, but not as restrictive), 11-15, 26-23, 8-11, 25-22, 18-25, 29-22.

The position is diagrammed.

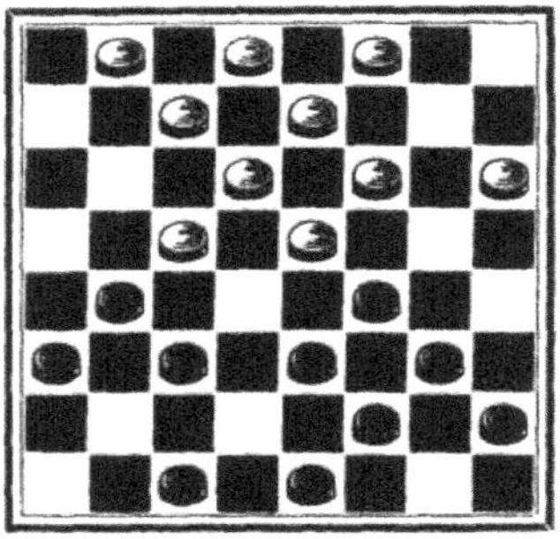

White to Play

F. 19-15, 10-19, 22-17, 6-10, 18-15, 11-18, 32-28, 10-15, 17-10, 9-14. Black wins.

G. 30-25 is an old draw line coming up from the Cross. White has to be careful because Black has a few tricks in store for him. Continuing 3-7, 32-28—H, 16-20, 18-15, 11-18, 22-15, 9-13, 19-16, 10-19, 27-24, 20-27, 31-15, 12-19, 23-16, 14-17, 21-14, 7-10, 14-7, 2-18, 16-11, 13-17, 11-7—J, 17-21, 26-22. Drawn—Published Play.

H. 27-24 loses by 16-20, 32-28, 20-27, 31-24, 11-16, 24-20, 7-11, 28-24, 9-13, 18-9, 5-14, 22-18, 6-9, 25-22, 2-6. Black wins.

J. White can be caught if he moves 25-21, 18-22, 21-14, 22-31, 28-24, 31-27, 24-19, 27-23, 19-15, 23-19, 14-10, 19-16, 10-1, 16-7, 1-6, 7-10. Black wins.

K. White can secure a hard draw by 30-25, 20-27, 31-24, 3-7, 24-20 (32-28 loses as in Note H), 11-16, 20-11, 7-16, 32-27, 16-20, 18-15, 2-7, 15-11, 7-16, 22-18, 10-15, 19-1, 16-19, 23-16, 14-30. Drawn.

L. 31-27 may lose by the cramp, e.g.: 11-16, 30-25, 3-7, 32-28, 9-13, 18-9, 5-14, 22-18, 14-17.

M. Going 22-18 is a trap as Black can now go 11-16, 18-9, 16-20 and Black should be able to force a win on the ending.

N. 28-24 goes out by 3-8 (11-15 is what White wants, then 21-17, 14-21, 23-18, 7-11, 18-14), 22-18—O, 14-17, 21-14, 10-17, 18-14, 17-22, 26-17, 13-22, 23-18, 6-10, 14-9, 10-14, 9-6, 14-23, 6-2, 7-10, 2-7, 10-15. Black wins.

O. M. Barrie defeated A. H. Jeffrey when the latter went 30-25, 11-15, 20-16, 13-17, 22-13, 15-18, 24-20, 18-27, 25-22, 8-11. Black wins.

P. 18-14 loses by 17-22, 26-17, 13-22, 23-18, 7-10. Black wins.

Q. Another loss is by 19-15, then 3-8, 28-24, 17-22, 26-17, 13-22, 24-19, 6-9 and Black is victorious.

R. 18-14 is another loss for White. Move 11-15, 16-12, 15-19 and Black wins.

S. White has made the only draw move. 16-12 also loses by 7-10, 28-24, 6-9, 24-19, 10-14, 19-15, 14-23, 15-8, 23-27, 8-4, 27-32, 4-8, 32-27, 8-11, 22-26, 30-23, 27-18, 20-16, 9-14, 11-8 and Black crowns the man on 14 and attacks the pieces in the single corner to win.

T. White has a slim draw by 18-14, 15-18, 14-9. Instead of 14-9 the writer has had players attempt to solve the problem by going 24-19 but they lose as follows: 22-26, 30-23, 18-27, 14-9, 27-31, 9-6, 31-27, 6-2, 27-23, 19-16, 23-18, 2-6, 18-15, 6-1, 15-10, 1-5, 10-6, 5-1, 6-2, 1-5, 7-10, 16-7, 2-11. Black crowns the piece he has on square 10, then brings him back to the middle of the board (all this time the king on square 11 stays there holding the two pieces). He then crowns the man on 3. With the king on 11 holding the two pieces his other two kings capture the lone white king.

Variation 1

The bust by 18-15, 11-18, 21-17, 14-21, 23-5, 16-23, 26-19 is often taken and brings out some fine play. I present an interesting game that the writer won giving a simultaneous blindfolded demonstration at Washington, D. C. in April, 1940. To continue:

3-7	32-28—D, E	12-26	19-16
25-22	6-9	30-23	23-19
7-11	24-20—F	21-25	16-12
31-26—A	11-15	22-18	1-6
6-9—C	20-16—G, H	25-30	10-1
26-23	15-24	18-15	19-10
2-6	28-19	30-26	12-8—J
27-24	10-15	23-19	Black
9-13	19-10	26-23	Wins

A. A popular White line published in many texts is as follows: 27-23, 6-9, 31-26, 2-6, 32-28 (if 23-18, 10-15 is published to win). 9-13, 28-24, 6-9, 22-18—B, 13-17, 24-20, 12-16, 19-12, 10-15, 26-22, 17-26, 23-19, 15-22 (the only jump as 15-24, 30-23 permits White to capture the man on 11 by moving 23-19, followed by 19-16 in the next few moves), 30-23, 9-14 (forced), 12-8, 22-26, 8-3, 26-31, 3-7, 31-27, 7-16, 27-18. Drawn.

B. In any of the games where my opponents went 23-18 I pitched 21-25, 30-21, 11-16, 26-23, 16-20 to an easy game.

C. Black can try to simplify matters by going 11-15, 27-24, and 2-7, arriving at a position R. Stewart drew with W. Stewart when the latter obtained this beautiful concealed stroke: 24-10, 15-24, 30-25, 21-30, 32-28, 30-23, 28-19, 23-16, 20-2 and the piece on 6 or 10 must fall.

D. 32-27 is tricky as Black would be forced to sacrifice a man to draw. Tescheleit offers this play: 13-17, 22-13, 11-15, 30-26 (as relinquishing the checker 23-18 is futile), 21-25, 26-22, 25-30, 23-18, 30-25, 18-11, 25-18, 11-7, 10-15, 19-10, 6-15, 7-2, 15-19, 24-15, 18-11, 27-23, 11-15, 23-19. Drawn.

E. 24-20 draws by 11-15, 32-28, 15-24, 28-19, 6-9, 22-18, 13-17, 18-15, 10-14, 15-10, 14-18.

F. A better move would be 23-18. Then 11-16, 19-15, 10-19, 24-15, 13-17. Drawn.

G. Black can win against 28-24 by 9-14, 20-16, 14-17, 23-18, 17-26, 18-11, 26-31, 24-20, 31-27.

H. 30-26 wins without any trouble as we can walk in for a king with the man on 21 and snare one of the pieces hanging by the wayside.

J. The win is apparent if we keep the king on square 10 which holds the piece on 5 and the king on 1. After crowning the pieces that we have on 9 and 13, we capture the remaining free man that is now located on 8.

Game 14

9-14, 22-18

9-14	18-9	10-14	22-18
22-18	13-22	17-10	11-15
5-9	26-17	7-14	18-11
25-22—1	6-22	29-25	14-18
11-16	30-26	4-8	23-14
24-19—2, 3, A	11-15	25-22	16-30
8-11	26-17	8-11	21-17
22-17—4, 5, 6	15-24	31-26—E, F	30-26
9-13—B	28-19—C	2-6—G	11-7
			Drawn

A. If 22-17, 9-13, 18-9, 13-22, 26-17, 6-22, 30-26, 10-15, 26-17, 16-19, 23-16, 12-19 Black is powerful.

B. This maneuver should be made to forestall White from moving 17-13 thereby stopping the cramp on Black's double corner.

C. A trap that many players fall into after taking the 27-11 jump is as follows: 7-16, 17-14, 10-17, 21-14, 16-19, 23-16, 12-19, 32-27, 4-8, 29-25, 8-11, 25-22, 11-15, 31-26—D, 3-7, 27-23 (22-17, 15-18 appears to draw now but very few resist going after the piece), 15-18, 22-15, 19-24, 28-19, 7-10, 14-7, 2-27, 26-22, 27-31, 22-17, 31-26, 17-14 (if 17-13, 1-5), 26-23, 19-16, 1-6. Black wins—a game won from non-book players many times.

D. Published play by J. Lees show us this draw line for White, but I have yet to meet the opponent who didn't move 31-26. Instead of 31-26, move 22-17, 3-7, 17-13, 1-5, 13-9, 7-10, 14-7, 2-11, 9-6, 19-23, 27-18, 15-22, 6-2, 11-15, 2-7, 15-18, 7-10, 18-23, 10-14, 23-26. Drawn.

E. Preparing to develop 26-22 later if necessary. If 22-18 is tried, then 1-5, 18-9, 5-14, confining White to only one move, 27-24, which loses. It would be too late to move 31-26 because of the two for one by 14-18. Black's power is located in the pieces on squares 11, 12, 14, and 16 which seems to hold all of White's pieces at bay. Continue after 22-18 (instead of the regular move—31-26) 1-5, 18-9, 5-14, 27-24, 16-20, 32-28 (if 31-27, 11-16, 19-15, 16-19 Black wins), 20-27, 31-24, and White shortly runs out of moves by 2-6, 24-20, 6-10, 28-24, 3-7. Black wins.

F. 27-24 is rickety for we move 16-20, 31-27 (22-18 or 22-17 loses on the same idea as Note E), 11-16, and White can squeeze out a hair line draw by 22-17, 2-7, 17-10, 7-14, 19-15, 16-19, 23-16, 12-28, 15-10, 14-18 (nothing better), 10-7, 3-10, 27-24, 20-27, 32-7. Drawn.

G. To stop the game from a quick climax I sometimes make a bid to win with this variation: 1-5, 22-18, 3-7, 18-9, 5-14, 26-22, 7-10, 22-18, 16-20, 18-9, 11-15, 27-24, 20-27, 23-18, 15-22, 32-23, 22-25, 21-17, 25-30, 23-18, 30-25, 17-13, 25-22, 18-15, 10-14, 9-6, 2-9, 13-6, 22-18, 15-11, 18-23, 19-15, 23-19, 15-10, 19-15, 11-7. A drawn game between Messrs. R. Stewart and J. Ferguson.

Variation 1

26-22 draws, but we try hard for a win if it is attempted.

26-22	22-17	21-14	27-18
11-15—A	9-13	10-17	31-26
18-11	18-9	25-21	18-15
8-15	13-22	17-22	26-23—C
24-19	9-5	18-14	32-27
15-24	6-9	22-26	23-32
28-19	30-25	23-18	15-10
7-11	22-26	16-23	32-27
22-18	31-22	14-10	21-17
11-16	9-14	7-14	27-23
25-22	22-18—B	18-9	17-13
3-7	14-17	26-31	23-18
		And 9-6—Drawn	

A. Another strong line for Black is 10-15.

B. R. T. Ward published this win if 22-17 is made: 7-11, 25-22, 11-15, 27-24, 16-20, 32-27, 4-8, 17-13, 2-6, 22-17, 8-11, 29-25, 15-18 and Black wins.

C. This game led into a position which Heffner drew against Moulding in the Second International. If 26-22 is made, the pitch by 29-25 draws on the theme as the above text.

Variation 2

29-25—A	10-19	23-16	2-7
8-11—B	24-15	12-19	11-2
18-15—C	16-19	32-27	9-13
11-18	23-16	1-5	2-9
22-15	12-19	15-11	5-32—G
10-19	31-27	14-18	Drawn
24-15	4-8	21-17—F	
7-10—E	27-23	18-22	
27-24	8-12	25-18	

A. Inferior, as Black is best in all the major variations with White adhering to a narrow path. The non-book performer's choice, often to his sorrow!

B. A strong line is 16-20, but the text is tricky.

C. The only draw move for White. The non-book player often becomes tangled here and falls into an early defeat. 24-19 loses and is like Variation 6. 24-20 is another loss. The writer has often won the following continuation: 24-20, 10-15, 27-24, 7-10, 24-19, 15-24, 28-19, 10-15, 19-10, 6-15, 32-28 (31-27 loses by 2-7, 27-24, 16-19, 23-16, 12-28), 2-6—D, 31-27, 16-19, 23-7, 14-32, 7-2, 1-5, 26-23, 9-13, 2-9, 5-14, 28-24, 32-28, 23-19, 3-8, 19-10, 28-19, 30-26, 12-16, 20-11, 8-15. Black wins.

D. 2-7 is deluding but White can escape by 22-17, 15-29, 17-10, 7-14, 30-25, 29-22, 26-10, 9-14, 28-24.

E. Black can vary his game almost at will but White must stay on the chalk-line.

F. Stanley Davis drew a game with us contested at West Chester, Pa., Y. M. C. A. by going 27-24, 18-23, 24-15 and my move was 3-7. In looking over the position we believe 23-27 offers us greater possibilities than 3-7.

G. May shock the opponent but the ending isn't strong enough to win.

Variation 3

18-15—A	1-6	28-19	14-17
10-19	25-22	15-24	9-14
24-15	6-10	22-18	17-21
7-10	21-17	24-27	14-17
27-24	16-19	18-9	22-25
10-19	23-16	27-31	17-22
24-15	12-19	9-6	25-29
2-7—B	27-24	31-22	20-16
31-27	10-14	6-2	21-25
8-11—C	17-10	11-15	16-11
15-8	7-14	2-6	25-30
4-11	24-20—E	22-26	11-7
22-17—D	3-7—F	23-18	30-25
9-13	32-27	15-22	23-18
17-10	7-10	30-23	25-21
6-15	27-23	10-14	7-2
29-25	19-24	6-9	21-17
			Drawn

A. An invitation is offered to complicate matters.

B. Rejecting the proposal and playing for simplification. 16-19 is the alternative and a worthwhile line. The play on 16-19 is voluminous and well known. When the play at A is offered I prefer making it a "rest" game and am satisfied with a draw.

C. Safety first.

D. 28-24, 6-10, 22-17, 9-13, 26-22, 16-20, 30-25, 3-8, and now White has the pressure on himself and Black forgets the initial aim for a simple draw and starts gunning for a win.

E. A point necessary to remember is that if White plays 32-27 you must play 11-16, 24-20, 13-17!!, 20-11, 14-18, 22-13, 18-23, 27-18, 15-31, 13-9, 31-27, 9-6, 27-23, 6-2, 23-18, 30-26, 18-15. Drawn—J. Robertson vs. A. Lambie.

F. "Stile's Manuscript" draws by 3-8, 32-27, 8-12, 27-23, 12-16, 30-25, 13-17, 22-13, 15-18, 25-21—G, 18-27, 26-22, 27-31, 22-17, 14-18, and plays 17-14 to an easy draw, but 13-9, 19-23, 9-6, 16-19, 6-2, 23-27, 2-7, leaves Black with a lot of pieces in the middle of the board with a position we don't relish.

G. "Stile's Manuscript" adds a touch of fireworks if 13-9, 18-27, 26-22—H, 27-31, 25-21, 31-26, 22-17, 26-23, 17-10, 11-15, 20-11, 19-24, 28-19, 23-5. Black wins.

H. White can draw by 25-22, 27-31, 9-6, 11-15, 20-11, 14-18, 6-2, 18-25, 26-22.

Variation 4

Black has the choice in this variation with many winning chances.

28-24	26-17	32-28	26-22
16-20	10-14—E	7-11	11-15
22-17—A,B,D	17-10	22-18	22-17
9-13	7-14	1-5	15-19
18-9	29-25	18-9	17-10
13-22	3-7—F	5-14	19-26
26-17	25-22	19-15	27-23
6-22	7-10	10-19—G	Drawn
30-26	31-26	24-8	
11-16—E	2-7	4-11	

A. Perfect timing is required to win for Black if 30-25 is made. Here is a game between George Dick and M. C. Priest: 11-15, 18-11, 7-16, 22-18, 4-8, 26-22, 1-5, 22-17, 9-13, 18-9, 5-14 (forcing White to make a weak waiting move), 32-28, 13-22, 25-9, 6-13, 29-25, 8-11, 25-22, 11-15, 21-17, 3-8, 31-26, 15-18, 22-6, 13-31, 6-1, 31-26, 1-5, 2-6, 5-1, 6-9, 1-6, 9-14. Black wins.

B. Published play shows us a win should 32-28 be taken: 11-16, 30-25, 4-8, 22-17, 8-11, 17-13—C, 11-15 (the combination idea to win is to dislodge the piece on 23 for the double to the king row) 18-11, 14-18, 23-5, 16-32, 11-8, 20-27, 31-24, 12-16, 8-4, 16-20. Black wins.

C. 25-22 loses for White by the same method as we can force White to jump out of 23. Move 25-22, 11-15, 18-11, 14-18, 22-15, 9-14, 11-8, 14-18, 23-14, 16-32, 15-11, 7-16, 14-7, 3-10. Black wins—G. Flynt.

D. 29-25 is a common loss as we can quickly win by cramping White's center. After 29-25, 4-8, 32-28, 11-16 the thrust by 16-19 or by 14-18 cannot be avoided.

E. Black has other alternatives but this has been the author's favorite in his serious encounters.

F. This is a key point. Remember that 3-7 should be made, and not 4-8.

G. A more involved and neater ending that I have adopted is jumping 11-18, 21-17, 14-21, 23-7, 21-25, 7-3, 25-30, 26-23, 30-25,

3-7, 4-8, 7-10, 25-22, 10-7—H, 8-11, 7-3—J, 11-15, 3-7—K, 16-19, 23-16, 12-19, 27-23—L, 19-26, 7-11, 20-27, 11-25. Drawn.

H. White can fall into this trap if he tries 10-15, 16-19, 23-16, 12-19, 15-10, 19-23. Black wins.

J. 7-10, 11-15, 10-19, 22-26. Black wins.

K. 23-18, 16-19, 18-11, 19-23, 27-18, 22-8, 24-19, 8-11. Black wins.

L. Only recently one of my opponents missed the point and did not pitch the man 27-23 to draw. He went 7-11, 22-18, 11-16, 19-23, 16-19, 23-32, 19-10, 20-27 and lost.

Variation 5

This line favors Black and forces White to do most of the work.

30-25	18-9	23-18—H	23-18
11-15	6-13	14-23	25-30
18-11	26-22	27-18	18-14
14-18	10-14	20-27	30-26
22-15	28-24	32-23	22-18
9-14	16-20	6-9	26-22
11-8—A	22-18	21-17	14-9
4-18	1-5	11-16	16-20
25-22—B	18-9	18-15	18-14
18-25	5-14	9-14	22-18
29-22	31-26	15-6	15-10
7-11	7-10—D	14-21	Drawn
22-18	26-22—E	19-15	
3-7—C	2-6	21-25	

A. Trying to hold the pieces works havoc with White: 26-22, 14-18, 23-14, 10-26, 31-22, 16-23, 27-18, 7-16, 32-27, 16-19, 18-14, 12-16, 21-17, 3-7, 25-21, 6-10, 15-6, 2-25, 29-22, 16-20 (the finishing touches on the game will be after we place men on 12 and 16, and taking two for one by 19-24), 17-14, 7-11, 14-10, 4-8, 10-7, 8-12, 7-3, 11-16, 3-7, 19-24. Black wins.

B. If 26-22, 10-15 (watch out for the trap if 3-8, 22-15, 7-11, 28-24, 11-18, 24-20, 8-11, 19-15, and White would win), 19-10, 6-15, 22-17. Black best.

C. Preventing a cramp on Black's double corner.

D. Published play on this game continues with Black going 13-17, 32-28, 14-18, 21-14, 7-10, 14-7, 11-16, 23-14, 16-32, 7-3, 20-27. Drawn.

E. 32-28, 11-16, 19-15—F, 10-19, 24-15, 2-6, 15-11, 6-10, 11-7—G, 10-15, 7-2, 15-19, 2-7, 14-18, 23-14, 19-24, 28-19, 16-32, 7-11 (or 26-22 easily drawn), 12-16, 26-23 (of course 11-7 is an easy draw), 32-27, 23-18, 20-24, 11-20, 27-32, 20-27, 32-23, 18-15, 23-18. Black wins by First Position.

F. 26-22, 13-17, 22-13, 2-6. Black wins.

G. 11-8, 10-15, 8-3, 15-18 (or 15-19 draws like Note E), 3-7, 13-17, 7-10, 18-22, 10-15, 22-31, 15-18, 31-24, 28-19, 20-24, 18-9, 17-22. Draws.

H. Black wins if 22-18, 6-9, 32-28, 13-17.

Variation 6

The non-book player invariably finds himself in a losing position when he moves 29-25.

4-8	23-14	11-16	21-17
18-15—A, B, C	9-18—F	27-23	5-9
11-18	31-26	18-27	17-13
22-15	16-23	32-23	9-14
1-5	26-19	3-7	Black wins
26-22—E	7-11	22-18	
14-18	30-26	7-11	

A. No escape for White whatever if he should attempt. Continue: 27-24, 16-20, 31-27, 11-16, 19-15—D, 10-19, 24-15, 7-11, 23-19 (for play on 22-17 see Trap sand Shots), 16-23, 26-19, 14-23, 27-18, 3-7, 22-17, 9-13 (not 11-16, 25-22, 16-23, 15-10), 17-14, 20-24, 30-26, 11-16, 26-23, 24-27, 14-10, 7-14, 18-9, 27-31, 25-22, 16-20, 23-18, 31-26, 9-5, 26-17, 21-14, 13-17, 32-27, 17-21, 27-23, 21-25, 14-10, 25-30. Black wins.

B. The game between A. Dyson and P. O'Neil exemplifies the win for Black should 21-17, 14-21, 18-15, 11-18, 23-5 be made. Continuing: 16-23, 26-19, 8-11, 27-23, 11-15, 28-24, 15-18, 22-15, 12-16, 19-12, 10-28, 25-22, 7-11, 22-18, 6-10, 31-26, 2-6, 26-22, 6-9, 22-17, 10-15, 17-13, 15-22, 13-6, 1-10, 5-1, 10-15, 1-6, 11-16, 6-10, 15-19, 23-18 and 22-26 takes away any hope of White securing a draw. Now supposing Black had moved 19-23 instead of 22-26, White might draw because of the man on 23 being subject to an attack, forming what is generally known as a bridge position (White on 30 and 32, Black on 23). Black's last move (22-26) broke the bridge position and an easy win follows.

C. 28-24 is crushed by 16-20, 32-28, 11-16, 19-15, 10-19, 24-15, 16-19, 23-16, 14-32. Black wins.

D. 18-15, 1-5, 22-18, 7-11, 26-22, 3-7, 30-26, 9-13, 18-9, 5-14, 22-18, 13-17, 18-9, 11-18, 21-14, 10-17, 23-14, 16-30. Black wins—Published Play.

E. Drummond has play for a Black win if 28-24 is tried. Move 16-20, 32-28, 7-11, 26-22, 11-18, 22-15, 3-7, 30-26, 7-11, 26-22, 11-18, 22-15, 2-7, 31-26, 7-11, 26-22, 11-18, 22-15, 9-13, 25-22, 5-9, 22-18, 13-17.

F. Instead of 9-18, we have been successful in jumping 16-23, 27-18, 10-19, to force a win but the other jump (9-18) makes the job easier.

Game 15

9-14, 22-17

9-14	18-9	16-23	13-9
22-17	5-14	31-27—D	16-19
11-16—A	29-25	3-7	18-14
24-19—1	16-20	27-18	11-16
8-11	25-22	7-16	22-18
25-22	11-16	30-26—H	19-23
11-15	22-17—3	20-24	26-19
17-13	7-11	17-14	16-23
15-24	26-22—B	10-17	14-10
28-19	11-15	21-14	12-16
4-8	23-18	6-10—J	Drawn
22-18—2	14-23—C	14-7	Published
8-11	27-11	2-11	Play

A. This forms the Pioneer. While White appears to have a slight edge in many variations of this game the opening is almost equal, with wins for both Black and White about on a par. The importance of this game lies in the fact that it is possible to transpose about fifty percent of all the openings into the Pioneer. With the exception of 9-13 and 10-14 all the opening moves can conceivably be run into Pioneer lines. A few examples of this type of transposition can be found in the Chapter of "Mid Game Structures." (See A Pioneer Pattern.)

B. A characteristic and important landing point of the Pioneer:

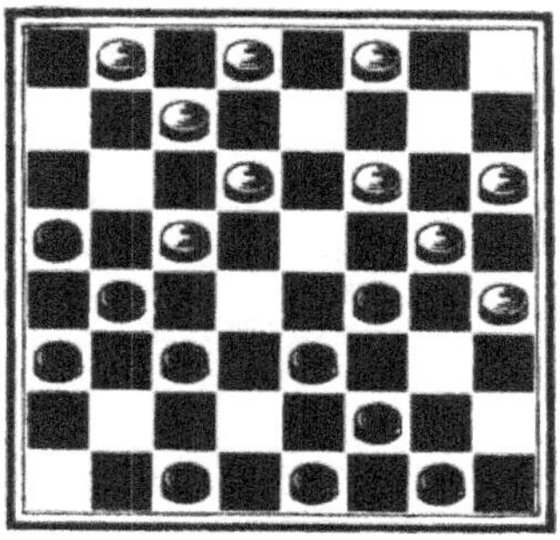

Black to Play

This position can come up in countless ways and is the transposition alluded to in Note A.

C. A tricky jump leading to many wins against the unwary. The other jump 15-24, 18-9 leads to a strong Black game and is used when playing those whom I feel know the pitfalls of the 14-23 jump.

D. The temptation to dart for a king by 11-8 has proven a nemesis to those unfortunate enough to try it. To win, play: 10-15—E, 8-4—F, 12-16, 17-14, 15-18, 22-15, 23-27, 32-23, 6-10, 14-7, 2-27, 31-24, 20-27, 21-17, 27-31, 17-14, 31-27, 14-10, 27-23, 13-9, 23-19, 9-6, 16-20, 6-2, 19-16, 2-7, 20-24. Black wins shortly.

E. The reason for not going 12-16 at this stage is that White would be able to move 31-27.

F. 31-27 loses by 15-18, 22-15, 23-26, 30-23, 6-9, 13-6, 1-26, 17-14—G, 12-16, 8-4, 26-30, 21-17, 30-26 (corrects J. T. Bradford, who plays 30-25 to a draw in the 9th American Tournament Book), 17-13, 2-6, 14-9, 6-10, 9-6, 10-15, 6-2, 15-19 and Black wins as White cannot save the man on 27.

G. 8-4, 12-16, 17-13, 26-30, 13-9, 30-26, 9-5, 26-22, 5-1, 16-19, 1-5, 2-7, 5-9, 7-11, 9-14, 3-8, 14-9, 8-12, 4-8, 11-16, 9-14, 22-26, 8-11, 19-24. Black wins.

H. Another draw for White is: 18-14, 10-15, 14-9, 15-19, 22-18, 19-23, 18-15, 16-19, 15-11, 12-16, 11-7, 2-11, 9-2, and now Black breaks White's bridge (men on squares 30 and 32 form bridge) by 23-26, 30-23, 19-26. Drawn—Martin vs. Adamson.

J. Black is preparing to line up pieces on squares 12, 16, and 19 to force an exchange of the man on 26, otherwise they will not be able to reach the king row without losing a man or run into a losing position.

Variation 1

25-22 is the choice of many players but avoided by the writer inasmuch as Black has the privilege of moving 16-19, to form what is known as the Double Corner Dyke. The break up, slightly in favor of Black, would force one to prepare for the employment of countless additional variations of book play.

25-22	15-18	31-24	23-16
8-11—A	30-25—C	16-20	14-7
22-18	11-16	25-22	3-10
16-20	24-19	20-27	6-2
18-9	2-7	22-18	16-11
5-14	26-22	6-9	17-14
29-25	7-11	13-6	10-17
11-15—B	22-15	27-31—E	21-14
25-22	11-18	18-9	11-15
7-11	27-24—D	31-27	9-5
17-13	18-27	23-18	Drawn
4-8	32-23	27-23	R. Griffen
22-17	20-27	18-14	vs. E. Ebert

A. Our preference in line with the Pioneer formation idea.

B. Beware of 4-8 which runs into Dunne's loss. This losing formation arises from different openings and must be known. Some years ago in playing with A. J. Mantell we ballotted the 11-16, 23-18 opening and not recognizing the subtle loss we fell an easy victim. (See Mid Game Structures—Dunne's Loss.)

C. White can vary with 24-19, 18-22, 19-16, 12-19, 23-7, 2-11, 26-23, 22-26, 23-18, 14-23, 27-18, 3-7 (not 25-29, 18-14, 29-25, 14-7, 3-10, 17-14 leaves Black in a precarious position), 17-14, 10-17, 21-14, 25-29, 18-15, 11-18, 14-9, 6-10, 9-6, 10-14, 6-2, 7-11, 31-26, 8-12, 32-27, 14-17, 26-22, 17-26, 30-14, 29-25, 14-10, 25-22. Drawn—Published Play.

D. Heffner and Barker continued with 31-26, 8-11, 19-15, 10-19, 17-10, 6-15, 23-14, 15-18, 26-22, 3-8, 22-15, 11-18, 14-10, 19-24, 28-19, 16-23, 10-7, 12-16, 7-3, 8-12, 3-7, 16-19, 7-10, 19-24. Drawn.

E. In a stake match with Charles Jolly, many times New Jersey champion, the writer varied with 1-5, and drew a hard fought game. Continuing 18-9, 5-14, 6-2, 27-31, 17-13 (Jolly improves on all published play), 8-11 (only move), 13-9, 31-26, 9-5, 26-22, 5-1, 3-8, 1-5, 22-18, 5-9, 18-27, 9-18, 27-24 (appears risky but is the only move I have to draw), 19-16, 12-19, 2-7, 11-16, 7-14, 24-27, 18-15, 27-23, 15-24, 16-20. Drawn.

Variation 2

The following line of play leads to an instructive mid game landing, known as Strickland's Draw.

29-25	26-19	28-19	22-17
8-11	3-8	10-15—F	2-6
22-17—A	30-26	19-10	26-22—H
11-15—B	8-11	6-15	14-18
25-22	26-23	17-10	23-14
15-24	5-9	9-14	6-9
27-11	32-28	13-9—G	Drawn
7-16	11-15	12-16	
23-19—E	31-26	9-5	
16-23	15-24	16-20	

A. A losing move often chosen by the uninformed is 22-18. In my exhibitions the win crops up regularly and is effected by: 10-15, 18-9, 15-24, 27-20, 5-14, 25-22, 16-19, 23-16, 12-19, 22-17, 7-10, 26-23, 19-26, 30-23, 11-15, 31-27 (if 20-16, 15-19, Black wins), 15-18, 27-24, 18-27, 32-23, 3-8, 23-19 (if 20-16, 14-18 Black wins), 8-12, 20-16, 2-7, 24-20, 14-18, 19-15, 10-19, 17-14, 6-10, 16-11, 10-17. Black wins—by Fairgrieve.

B. Black can vary by 16-20, securing the better position. The text (11-15) is restrictive and instructive. My suggestion would be to first learn the above draw as the position occurs from many other openings and should prove useful. The powerful alternative for Blacks continues, after 16-20:

19-16—C	17-10	22-17	11-8
12-19	7-14	13-22	3-12
23-16	16-11	26-10	10-7
11-15	19-24	5-9	15-19
26-23	13-9	31-26	23-16
15-19	6-13	9-14	12-19
30-26	25-22—D	26-22	7-2
10-15	24-28	2-6	

And now be sure to go 6-10, then after 27-24 the draw is assured (H. Jacob).

C. A likely looking move might be 25-22. Now we can quickly see that if 11-16, 22-18, 7-11, we can transpose the position into the trunk game of this opening. Here we must resist the convenience of relying on our knowledge and see if Black has a better move. The follow-up by 11-15, 19-16, 12-19, 23-16, 15-19, 30-25, 5-9, 32-28, 20-24, 27-20, 7-11, 16-7, 2-11, 31-27, 10-15, 17-10, 19-24, 28-19, 15-31, 10-7, 3-10, 26-23, 10-14, 23-19, 11-15, 19-10, 6-15, 13-6, 1-10, 22-17, 31-26, 25-22, is suggestive of the problematical draw White has to find—F. Hagen.

D. A loss is in store for White if he should try to win by 32-28 as it boomerangs with 15-18, 28-19, 14-17, 21-14, 5-9, 14-5, 3-7, 23-14, 7-30, 25-21, 30-25, 14-10, 25-22, 27-23, 20-24, 23-19, 22-18. 19-16, 18-15. John Robertson beat James Wylie.

E. Holds the pressure, otherwise Black can safely cut 16-19.

F. This position should be in every player's "must" as it is a defensive key. We diagram it for you.

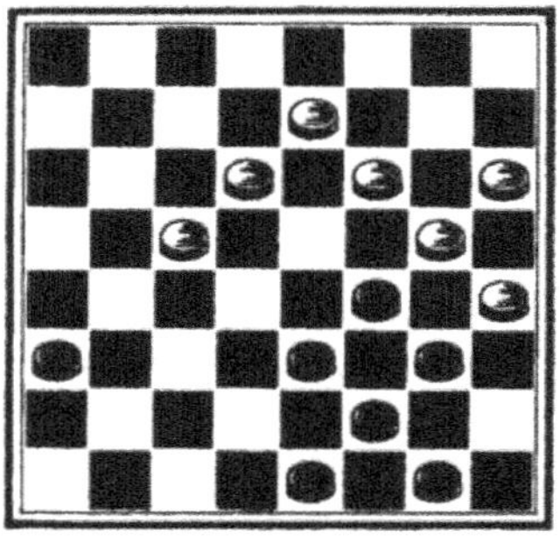

Black to Move and Draw

G. If 22-17, 2-6, 26-22 (if 10-7, 15-18, 17-10, 18-27 etc. draws), 12-16, 10-7, 15-19, 17-10, 19-26, 7-2, 6-15, 2-7, 16-20, 7-11, 15-19 Drawn.

H. If 10-7, 15-18, 17-10, 18-27. Drawn.

Variation 3

Willie Ryan (White) and the writer reached this position in the final heat in the 1933 New York Masters' Tournament. Willie needed only a draw to clinch the heat and win first prize. Despite the use of a "cook" on my part that is just what he did. Our continuation follows:

22-18	10-15	18-14—E	3-8
14-17	18-2	22-17	5-1
21-14	1-5	14-9—F	8-11
10-17	2-9	17-14	2-6
26-22—A	5-30	9-5	11-15
17-26	19-15	14-18—G	6-9
31-22	30-26—C	15-10	12-16
7-10	23-19	18-14	9-5
22-17—B	16-23	10-6	16-19
2-7	27-18	14-10	13-9—H
30-25	26-22—D	6-2	Drawn

A. White has only a narrow draw after this move; 18-14 is preferred. The following play is from a game played between Willie Ryan and Walter Hallman in the 2nd N. C. A. Tourney: 18-14, 1-5, (steering clear of 7-11, the book move which Hallman had "cooked" up as a loss for this tourney) 19-15, 16-19, 23-16, 12-19, 32-28, 17-22, 26-17, 6-9, 13-6, 2-18, 15-11, 7-16, 27-23, 18-27, 31-15. Drawn.

B. 30-25 now would be out of order and would allow the following spectacular win: 3-7, 22-17, 10-14, 18-9, 7-10 (threatening 10-14), 23-18, 16-23. Black wins handily.

C. A big improvement over published play where 16-19 is played to draw.

D. Maintains the grip.

E. White might play for a man down draw at this stage, but as Ryan pointed out this would prove fatal: 13-9, 22-26, 9-6, 26-23, 6-2, 23-14, 15-10, 14-7, 2-11, 12-16, 11-15, 16-19, 15-24, 20-27, 32-23, 3-7, 23-18, 7-10. Black wins.

F. Only move to draw and varies from the win I had mapped out if 15-10, the move I was playing for. It loses as follows: 15-10, 12-16, 13-9, 17-22, 9-5, 22-18, 14-9, 18-14, 10-6, 14-10, 5-1, 3-8, 6-2, 8-11, 2-6, 11-15, 9-5, 16-19, 6-2 and Black proceeds to get all kings, something White cannot prevent. Note how the White forces are all tangled up in the double corner. The basis for the Black win is the Double Corner Block (see Lesson No. 1 in the End Game Section). The main thing is to keep the king stationed on square 10. This powerful monarch which has the protection of the single man on 15 (later becoming a king) holds the White king on 1 and the piece on 5 until the final victory is achieved. After having crowned all Black's pieces proceed as follows: (Black now has kings on 10, 15, 19, and 20), 19-24, 32-28, 24-19, 2-6, 20-24, 6-9, 15-11, 9-13 (if 9-6, 11-7 Black wins), 11-7, 13-9, 7-2, 9-13, 24-27, 13-9, 27-23, 9-13, 23-18, 13-9, 18-22, 9-13, 2-6. Black wins.

G. 3-8, 5-1, 12-16, 32-28 (the saving link), 16-19, 1-6. Drawn.

H. Thus Mr. Ryan won the City Championship for the year 1933.

Game 16

9-14, 23-18, 14-23

9-14	14-23	4-8	16-19
23-18—A	26-12	25-22	23-16
14-23	11-15	9-13	14-23
27-18—B	25-22	31-27	16-11
12-16—C	8-11	2-6	6-10
18-14	29-25	27-23	11-4
10-17	1-6	11-16	10-19
21-14	24-19	30-25	4-8
6-9—D	15-24	5-9—F	23-26
14-10—E	28-19	25-21—G	22-18
7-14	6-10	10-14	26-31
22-18	22-18	19-15—J	8-11

Drawn—Sam Gonotsky

A. This is the weakest of all the seven replies that White has to 9-14 with the exception, of course, of 21-17, which is an outright loss. This is one of the so-called "Barred Openings" although it is tenable and included among the three movers. The basic weakness of the White game is the "hole" in the mid-section created by the exchange via 23-18. Any exchange that takes men off squares 26 and 27 should be avoided. 11-16, 23-19 is another illustration of bad exchanging in the opening and one that leaves White with a total wreck. The difference between exchanges like 24-19 and 22-18, which are quite right at the start of the game, and 23-18 and 23-19 is that the former type leaves White's game *intact* while the latter disorganizes his forces at the beginning of hostilities.

B. Time and analysis have proven 26-19 to be a probable loss, when followed by 11-15.

C. This and 5-9 constitute the main lines of attack, with text having a slight edge over the latter.

D. Any other move at this point would allow White an even game.

E. This double exchange forms the basis of White's draw.

F. Text is correct as 6-9 or 8-11 would let White off easy. For example: 6-9, 25-21, 8-11, 32-28, 10-14, 12-8, 3-12, 19-15, etc. Drawn.

G. At this point E. C. Waterhouse played 18-15 against L. M. Lewis in the 6th American Tourney and the following play ensued: 18-15, 10-14, 25-21—H, 3-7, 12-3, 7-10, 19-12, 10-26, 3-7, 26-30, 7-11, 30-25, 22-17, 13-22, 12-8, 22-26, 11-15, 26-31, 8-3, 9-13, 3-7, 6-9, 7-2, 25-22, 2-6, 14-18, 15-19, 9-14, 6-9, 22-26, 19-15, 18-22, 9-25, 13-17, 21-14, 31-27, 32-23, 26-17. Black wins.

H. The following play by A. J. Heffner sustains the White draw: 22-18, 13-17, 32-28, 16-20, 19-16, 17-22, 15-10, 6-15, 18-4, 22-29, 4-8, 29-25, 8-11, 25-22, 23-19, 22-18, 19-15, 18-23, 15-10. Drawn.

J. 18-15, 3-7, 12-3, 7-10, 19-12, 10-26 wins for Black as in note G.

Game 17

9-14, 23-19

9-14	15-24	8-11	1-5—L
23-19	28-19	31-26—D	20-16
11-15	11-15	10-14	11-27
22-17	27-24	19-10	19-15
6-9—A	14-17	14-23	10-19
17-13	21-14	26-19	17-1
2-6	9-18	7-14	9-14
25-22	26-23	25-21—H	1-6
8-11	18-27	3-7	14-18
29-25	32-23	22-17—K	6-10
4-8	5-9—B	7-10	Drawn
24-20	23-18—C	30-25	

A. Forms the Souter opening brought up more often from 11-15, 23-19, 9-14, 22-17, 6-9.

B. Played in the 19th Century but neglected by the modern text books. This move is tricky leading to wins galore.

C. 25-21, 9-14, 21-17, 14-21, 23-18, 7-11, 31-26, 3-7, 18-14, 10-17, 19-3, and 11-15 effectively ties up the White forces. Published Play.

D. The old standard line was played as follows: 20-16, 11-27, 18-2, 27-32, 2-7, 10-14, 7-11, 32-28, 19-15, 14-18, 22-17—E, 28-24, 30-26—F, 24-28, 17-14, 28-24, 14-5, 6-9, 13-6, 1-19. Drawn—Sturges.

E. 15-10, 6-15, 13-6, 1-10, 11-7—G, 18-23, 7-14, 15-18, 22-15, 23-27, 31-24, 28-17. Black wins—W. Hay.

F. If 25-21, 24-20, 17-14, 18-23, 14-5, 6-9, 13-6, 1-19, 11-15, 20-24, 15-18, 23-27. Drawn—Drummond's reprint.

G. Here is where the draw was missed: 22-17, 18-22, 25-18, 15-22, 11-7, 10-15, 7-10, 15-19, 10-14, 19-23, 14-18, 23-27. Drawn—Spayth.

H. White would lose if he moved 19-15, by 11-18, 22-15, 14-18, 25-22, 18-25, 30-21, 9-14, 15-11—J, 14-18, 11-8, 18-23, 8-4, 23-27, 4-8, 27-32, 8-11, 32-28, 24-19, 28-24, 11-15, 6-10, 15-6, 1-10. Black wins—Drummond's reprint.

J. 24-19, 14-18, 21-17, 3-7, 20-16, 18-23, 15-11, 7-10, 11-7, 10-14. Black wins—Drummond's reprint.

K. 30-26 loses by 1-5, 22-17, 7-10, 26-23, 11-15, 20-16, 15-18, 16-11, 18-27, 24-20, 14-18. Black wins.

L. 11-15, 20-16, 15-18, 16-11, 18-22, 25-18, 14-23, 11-7, 23-27, 7-2, 1-5, 2-7, 27-32, 7-14, 9-18, 19-15, 32-27, 17-14, 27-20, 14-10. Drawn—J. McFarlane.

Game 18

9-14, 24-19

9-14	18-15—1	11-16	2-7
24-19	11-18	18-15	12-16
11-15	21-17	20-24	22-17—F
22-18	14-21	15-6	9-13
15-24	23-5	2-9	17-14
18-9	4-8	23-18	19-23
5-14	29-25	16-23	14-10
28-19	8-11	26-19	23-14
8-11	25-22	24-27	7-2
25-22	3-8—B	19-15	14-7
11-15	22-18	27-31	2-20
32-28	11-16	15-10	13-17
15-24	27-23	31-27	Drawn
28-19	8-11	10-7	Harold
7-11	26-22	27-24	Freyer
22-18	16-20	7-2	
6-9—A	31-26—E	24-19	

Notes by Harold Freyer

A. Not as well covered by published play as 1-5, therefore there is more room for original play.

B. Adopted by Harold Freyer against H. O. Newcomb at the national tournament for the American Championship at Martins Ferry, Ohio, in 1937. It is off published play. Ryan's "It's Your Move" gives: 11-16—C, 26-23—D, 3-8, 27-24, 16-20, 23-18, 20-27, 31-24, 8-11, 24-20, 2-6, 19-16, 12-19, 18-14, 10-26, 30-7. Drawn.

C. Denvir's Two Move Guide gives 11-15, 27-24, 3-7, 26-23, 2-6, 22-17, 7-11, 17-13, 11-16, 24-20, 15-24, 20-11, 10-15, 11-7, 12-16, 7-2, 15-18, 23-14, 6-9, 13-6, 1-17. Drawn—Denvir vs. Bradford.

D. In a game with Harold Freyer, Monte Schleifer played 27-23, 16-20, 31-27, 3-8, 22-18, 8-11, 19-15, 10-19, 23-7, 2-11, 26-23, 12-16, 18-15, 11-18, 23-14, 16-19. Drawn.

E. This combination move enables White to force a series of exchanges which simplifies the position.

F. To here as contested between Freyer and Newcomb where Newcomb played 7-10, 16-20, 22-17, 20-24, 10-7, 9-13, 17-14, 19-23, 7-11, 13-17, 18-15, 23-18, 14-9 (14-10 draws outright) now Freyer played 17-22 (18-14 makes White play cautiously to draw).

Variation 1

The following is a more confining line:

26-22—A	22-18	25-22	18-15
3-8	15-22	14-17	12-16
27-24—B	25-18	21-14	Etc.
1-5—C	9-13	10-26	Drawn
30-25	18-9	31-22	Denvir
11-15	5-14	7-10	vs. Lewis
18-11	29-25	22-18	
8-15	2-7	4-8	

A. Black plays for 29-25 then 12-16, 19-12, 10-15.

B. In a game between Freyer and Herman, Herman played 22-17, 11-15, 18-11, 8-24, 27-20, 4-8, 29-25, 9-13, 25-22, 8-11, 22-18, 13-22, 18-9, 22-25, 9-5, 10-14, 31-26, 25-29, 23-19, 29-25, 26-22, 25-18, 19-15, 11-16, 20-11, 12-16. Freyer won.

C. Now it's White's turn to set a trap. **11-15, 18-11, 8-15,** loses by **21-17, 14-21, 23-18.** Denvir's Guide.

Game 19

9-14, 24-20, 5-9

9-14	30-26—F	3-7	22-15
24-20—A	6-10	18-14—J	7-10
5-9—B	22-18	12-16—K	14-7
22-18	1-5	32-28—L	2-18
10-15—1	18-9	15-19—M	31-26
28-24—C	5-14	24-15	4-8
15-22	26-22	11-25	Drawn
26-10—D	10-15	20-11	F. Dunne
7-14	23-18—G	8-15	
25-22	14-23	29-22	
9-13—E	27-18	15-18	

A. An even game with chances for new explorations.

B. Safest; 6-9, 10-15, 11-15 and 11-16 can also be played broadening the scope of the opening.

C. 25-22 may tie up White, because of 7-10, with the idea of playing 3-7 and 1-5 next.

D. White's apex piece (26) goes, but so does Black's (7).

E. An old line revitalized by L. T. deBearn.

F. If 22-18, 6-9 is good for Blacks.

G. If 24-19, 15-24, 22-18, 13-17—H, 18-9, 17-22, 32-28, 3-7, 28-19, 22-26, 31-22, 11-16, 20-11, 8-31. Drawn.

H. 14-17, 21-14, 24-28, 14-9, 11-16, 20-11, 8-22 wins a piece but is hard to handle in view of 9-5, 3-7, 5-1, 7-10, 1-5, 4-8, 5-9, 8-11, and at this point published play is 23-19 and the continuation favors Black. Harold Freyer suggests 9-5 (a good waiting move) and it appears to place the laboring oar on Black.

J. Black should be able to win if 31-26, or 32-28 is played by moving 11-16.

K. The clearance is in sight.

L. 14-9 permits 16-19, 32-28, 19-23, giving us control of the game.

M. Carrying out the idea behind 12-16 at Note K.

Variation 1

We present an innovation on the popular 11-16, 20-11, 8-22, 25-18 line with the White Side, as shown to us by the late Mike Lieber.

4-8	1-5	12-16—E	10-15—H
29-25—A	32-27	23-19	12-8
8-11	9-13	16-23	21-25—H
28-24	18-9	26-19	30-21
10-15	5-14	13-17	22-26
25-22	21-17—C	22-6	31-22
7-10—B	14-21	2-9	15-19
24-20	23-18	19-16	24-15
3-7	6-9—D	15-22	11-25
27-24	27-23	16-12	Drawn

A. 28-24, 8-11, 24-19, 11-16 and we are in the trunk of Game 13.

B. A model game on 6-10 would be continued: 24-20, 1-5, 27-24, 9-13, 18-9, 5-14, 32-28, 11-16, 20-11, 7-16, 24-19, 15-24, 28-19, 3-8, 22-18, 8-11, 18-9, 11-15, 21-17, 15-24, 23-18, 13-22, 26-17, 16-20, 17-13, 10-14, 31-26 as drawn by G. Jewitt vs. C. Powell.

C. The move that opens up new territory. There are not many winning chances with this sacrifice, if Black will accept an easy draw. In matches or tourneys, we prefer to have our opponents on our own grounds, giving them a chance to over-play a position.

D. Black can pitch the piece 13-17, 22-13, 15-22, 26-17, 11-15, 27-23, 15-19, 24-15, 10-26, 31-22 (Drawn) to a quick climax. Black may not feel obliged to return the gift and may try to keep it.

E. Moving 2-6, 23-19 with the idea of giving the piece up by 13-17, 22-13, 15-22, 26-17 makes Black's position precarious. Continuing: 11-15—F, 20-16, 9-14—G, 24-20, 15-24, 16-11, 7-16, 20-11, 14-18, 11-7, 10-15, 7-2 and disaster for Black looms ahead.

F. Black is also in trouble if 9-14 should be tried for 19-15, 11-18 (10-28, 17-3 may win), 24-19, 18-22, 19-15, 10-19, 17-3, 19-24, 3-7, 22-25, 7-2, 6-10 and the White king is too strong to be stopped.

G. 15-18, 24-20, 18-22, 31-27, 9-14, 27-23, 22-26, 19-15 Black's downfall is apparent.

H. Clearing the position as it is too risky to keep the man with so many loose pieces in the middle of the board.

Game 20

9-13, 22-18, 12-16

9-13—A	6-10—G	7-10—M	13-22
22-18—B	29-25	14-7	7-2
12-16—C	10-17	2-11	5-9—N
24-20	21-14	27-24	2-6
8-12	1-6	20-27	9-14
27-24	25-21	31-8	6-10
3-8	6-10	4-11	14-17
25-22—D	32-27	18-14	10-15
16-19—E	10-17	11-15	17-21
24-15	21-14	14-10	28-24
10-19	8-12—H	15-18	22-25
23-16	20-16—L	10-7	24-19
12-19	11-20	18-22	25-29
18-14—F	22-18	26-17	Drawn

A. Forms the Edinburgh, which is the weakest opening move at Black's command.

B. The strongest attack.

C. During the two move era, 12-16 was the most popular line of the Edinburgh for the reason that it partly offsets the weakness of Black's double corner.

D. This move is passed over lightly in different checker books with a note that after Black plays 16-19, the game is equal. This game is given to prove the fallacy of that statement.

E. Forced: 5-9, a possible alternative loses by 24-19, 11-15, 18-11, 8-24, 28-19, 7-11, 30-25, 10-15, 19-10, 6-15, 22-18, 15-22, 25-18, 2-6, 32-27. White wins.

F. A powerful move that puts Black on the defensive. The man on 14 is well posted and is a constant threat.

G. 6-9, 14-10, 7-14, 22-17, 13-22, 26-10, 11-16 may lead to a hair line draw for Black.

H. 2-6 loses by 30-25, 6-9—J, 27-24, 9-18, 24-15, 5-9, 31-27, 9-14, 15-10, 14-17, 10-3, 17-21, 3-12, 21-30, 22-8. White wins.

J. If 11-15, 25-21, 6-9, 14-10, 7-14, 22-17, 13-22, 26-10, 9-14—K, 10-7, 14-18, 31-26, 8-12, 20-16, 5-9, 7-2, 9-13, 2-7, 18-22, 26-17, 13-22, 16-11, 12-16, 7-10, 16-20, 10-7. White wins.

K. 19-24, 28-19, 15-24, 10-7, 24-28, 27-23, 28-32, 7-3, 8-12, 3-7, 32-28, 7-10, 28-24, 10-6, 9-13, 6-10, 24-28, 10-15, 28-24, 23-18. White wins.

L. In tracing the game I find that Shearer offers 27-23, 4-8, 23-16, 12-19, 26-23 (given as the only move), 19-26, 30-23. Drawn. The pitch, 20-16, 11-20, given in the trunk, seems to be the combination that was missed.

M. The strength of White's position is apparent. We diagram the setting before 7-10 is made:

Black to Play

We deem it advisable to discuss the means by which the expert arrives at the correct move.

The combination of two methods may be used in finding the correct move in any given position. The experienced player employs his developed judgment and immediately considers the move which appears to be best. He follows it through to its final stages. In other words to the climax and subsequent clearance.

However, sometimes a position is so complicated that even top-notch players cannot follow through to the end in the five minute time limit. In such a case the system used is known as the "process of elimination." Most players use this method without even realizing it, though they do not get the same results as the expert who goes about it in a really scientific manner. The seasoned player considers all playable moves but discards one by one the moves he deems unsatisfactory until only one or two remain. These he gives his utmost attention and selects the one that has survived the most thorough and critical examination. In this final analysis it is the player's own judgment gained from long experience that ultimately decides the fate of the game.

13-17 and 2-6 seem to lose by 27-24. If 12-16 at the diagrammed position a draw might ensue but it is likely to be missed in a game. The following variation is probable continuation: 12-16, 27-24, 20-27, 31-15, 16-19 (7-11 may draw), 15-10, 7-11, 10-7, 11-16, 7-3, 16-20, 14-10, 20-24, 10-7, 2-11, 3-7, 11-16, 26-23, 19-26, 28-12, 26-31, 7-10, 31-26, 10-14. White wins.

4-8 is another hard draw at the diagram. Play 27-24, 20-27, 31-15, 7-11, 28-24, 11-16, 24-19, 15-24, 26-19, 13-17, 14-10, 5-9, 10-6, 2-7, 6-2, 7-11, 15-10, 9-14, 18-9, 11-15. Drawn.

Another loss at the diagram is 20-24, 27-20, 4-8, 18-15, 7-10, 14-7, 2-18, 26-23, 19-26, 31-15, 5-9, 28-24, 9-14, 24-19, 14-18, 20-16, 18-23, 16-11. White wins.

A difficult win at the diagrammed position would be against 7-11. This loses by 27-24, 20-27, 31-8, 4-11, 14-10, 11-16, 18-15, 5-9, 15-11, 9-14, 11-8, 14-18, 26-22, 18-25, 30-21, 16-19, 8-4, 19-23, 4-8, 23-27, 8-11, 27-32, 28-24, 32-28, 11-15, 28-19, 15-24, 12-16, 24-20, 16-19, 20-16, 19-23, 16-11, 23-27, 10-7, 27-31, 7-3, 31-27, 11-15, 27-23, 3-8, 23-27, 15-19. White wins.

N. Black must still be careful. If 12-16, 2-6, 16-20, 6-10, 5-9, 10-15, 9-14, 15-19, 14-17, 19-23, 22-26, 23-27, 26-31, 28-24, 17-21, 27-23, 20-27, 23-32. White wins.

Game 21

9-13, 22-18, 6-9

9-13	24-20	14-18*	14-9
22-18	8-11—A	23-14	27-23
6-9	27-24—B	16-23	9-6
26-22	3-7	24-19	23-16
1-6	24-19	2-6*—D	26-23
30-26	9-14	28-24	10-15
11-15	26-22	23-27	6-2
18-11	6-9	31-26	16-19
8-15	28-24	27-32	23-16
22-17	9-13	25-22	12-28
13-22	22-18	32-27	20-16
25-11	13-17	22-13	11-20
7-16	18-9	10-17	2-18—F
29-25—1	5-14	21-14	Drawn
4-8—2, 3	32-28	6-10	Long vs. Freyer

A. 16-19 loses by: 23-16, 12-19, 27-23, 8-12, 23-16, 12-19, 32-27, 3-8, 27-23, 8-12, 23-16, 12-19, 31-27, 10-14, 27-24, 19-23, 26-19, 9-13, 19-15, 14-18, 20-16, 6-9, 16-11, 9-14, 11-7, 2-11, 15-8, 13-17, 8-3, 17-22, 3-7. White wins—W. T. Dailey.

5

B. 26-22 was given to win by Richard Fortman, but the following game played between W. T. Dailey (Black) and Newell W. Banks was given to prove that it only draws: 26-22, 9-13, 27-24, 3-7—C, 24-19, 10-14, 28-24—D, 6-10, 22-18, 13-17, 18-9, 5-14 now the same position as the trunk between Long and Freyer at the 30th move, where Freyer played 32-28 which is stronger than 25-22, 17-26, 31-22, 11-15, 20-11, 7-16, 24-20, 15-24, 20-11, 24-27, 22-18, 27-31, 18-9, 31-26. Drawn.

C. Corrects Fortman who plays 10-15, 24-19, 15-24, 28-19, 6-10, 22-18, 3-7, 25-22. White wins—Dailey's note.

D. 22-18 is met by 6-10 and Black gets an easy draw. Dailey.

E. The only move to draw. W. T. Dailey gave 11-15 followed by 20-16, but 14-9, 15-24, 28-19 and Black has no waiting move. White wins. I had hoped Asa would make this 11-15 but he saw it would lose. Harold M. Freyer.

F. The notes of the Trunk and Variation 1 were kindly submitted by Harold Freyer.

Variation 1

The following game on 24-20, "the Case vs. Rubin line" was played between Harold Freyer (Black) and Abe Herman of New York City:

24-20	22-17	14-10	23-19
3-8	13-22	11-15—A	13-22
20-11	26-17	31-26—B	19-10
8-15	6-9	5-9	etc.
29-25	17-14	10-6	Drawn
4-8	10-17	18-22*	
25-22	21-14	26-17	
8-11	9-18	9-13	
28-24	23-14	27-23	
9-13	15-18	2-9	

A. Published play goes 18-22, 27-23, 11-16, etc. Drawn. This 11-15 avoids any possibility of an ending. Harold Freyer.

B. 27-23, 18-27, 32-23, 5-9, 10-6, 9-14, 6-1, 15-18, 24-19, 18-27, 31-24, 14-18, 24-20, 18-23, 19-15, 23-26. Drawn. Published play from a different order of moves by Fred Werner.

Variation 2

In preparing for the 10th American Tourney the following line was "cooked up" for any of my opponents who might attempt playing this accepted variation (10-14). The move had been chosen by many of the leading players as the standard draw and was published as such. After seeing Long play 4-8 at the tourney, the writer realized his chances of snagging any of the top experts were considerably lessened and submitted this game to the American Checkerist:

10-14	25-21	18-23	12-8
24-20	4-8	2-7	26-31—F
3-8	26-23	14-18	8-3
20-11	12-16	13-9	31-26
8-15	24-20	21-25	3-8
26-22	8-11	9-6	26-31
14-18	21-17	25-30	11-16
23-14	14-21	7-11	27-23
9-18	23-14	30-26	8-11
28-24	15-18	6-2	31-26
2-7	14-9	23-27	7-10
21-17	6-10	2-7	26-30
7-10—A	9-6—B	27-31	10-14
31-26	16-19—C	20-16	30-26
5-9	32-28—E	26-23	14-17
17-14	11-15	24-20	26-31
10-17	27-24	23-27	17-22
22-13	10-14	16-12	White wins
9-14	6-2	31-26	K. M. Grover

A. Play was originally given on 4-8, 17-14, 6-10, the annotator continuing 31-26, overlooking the simple two for two by 14-9, 5-14, 24-19, as pointed out by Walter Hallman. R. B. Cornell of Youngstown, Ohio, then temporarily sustained the draw by introducing 7-10 as given here.

B. The diagram sets the position before 9-6, the improved move, is made.

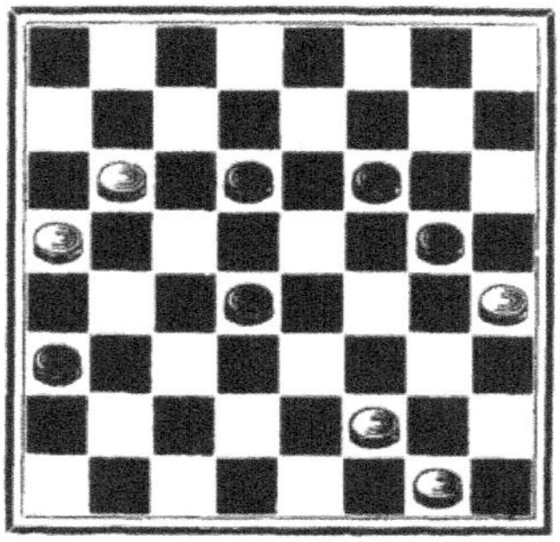

White to Play and Win

Robert Cornell gave 27-24 here, which only draws.

C. If 18-22, 6-2, 22-26, 32-28, 10-14, 2-7, 14-18. 13-9, 26-30—D, 27-24, 30-26, 7-3, 18-22, 3-8. White wins.

D. 18-22, 7-3. White wins.

E. The waiting move that cinches the win. If 6-2, then 10-15 draws. This appears to be the point where Cornell misjudged his analysis.

F. 19-23, 8-3, 26-22, 7-10, 15-19, 11-15, 27-24, 10-14. White wins.

Variation 3

During the 9th Tourney Ryan and Long found the win if 9-14 is made at this juncture. Prior to this tournament published play gave this move to draw. Finding no draw on this line, the analysts thought 10-14 would be safe. Variation 2 shows the win on 10-14. The consensus of opinion regards 4-8 the only tenable move. The critics are trying to find a loophole in the line and it is possible that a new draw will have to be discovered even though the move has withstood incessant hammering by the experts to date.

9-14	20-16	14-17	15-18
24-20	12-19	9-6	25-30
3-8	23-16	17-22	18-23
20-11	14-17—B	6-2	8-11
8-15	21-7	22-25	31-27
25-22	2-20	2-7	11-15
6-9—A	22-17	25-30	28-24
28-24	13-22	7-10	30-25
9-13	26-17	30-25—C	23-26
24-19	5-9	10-15	25-30
15-24	17-13	25-22	26-22
27-20	9-14	32-28	White wins
4-8	13-9	22-25	

Ryan and Long—9th Tourney Book

A. Gene Zuber played 4-8 against me in the 10th American Tourney and after 22-17 his game soon become hopeless.

B. Two days after the 9th American Tourney Willie Ryan and Newell W. Banks reached this position from a different opening and Mr. Banks played 2-6 and lost as follows: 2-6, 16-12, 8-11, 32-27, 11-16, 12-8, 16-20, 8-3, 14-18, 22-15, 10-19, 26-23. White wins.

C. If 8-11, then 10-14, 11-15, 14-17, 15-18, 31-27. White wins—Long.

Game 22

9-13, 22-18, 10-15

The following improvement of published play is submitted by Norman H. Clark, well known critic and analyst of Bangor, Maine. All notes are by Mr. Clark:

9-13	13-22	9-13	15-18
22-18	26-10	23-18	9-6
10-15	7-14	13-22	3-7
25-22	30-26	27-23	6-1
6-10	15-22	10-15	7-10
24-20	26-10	23-19	Forms position
5-9	2-7	7-10	on diagram:
28-24	10-6	32-27	
10-14	1-10	10-14	
22-17	21-17	18-9	

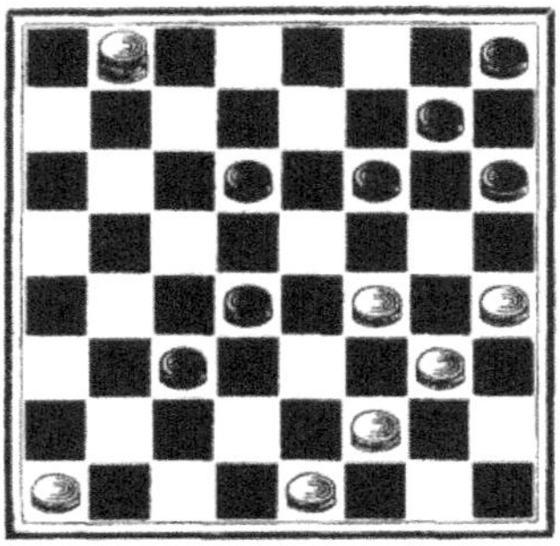

White to Play, Black Draws

20-16*—A	14-17—C	19-15	8-12*
11-20	10-14	12-16*	7-3
1-6	8-11*	15-10	16-19
10-14—B	14-21*	11-15*	21-17
6-10	4-8*—D	10-7	Drawn
			N. H. Clark

A. Improves play in Kear's Encyclopedia where 1-6, then 11-15 etc. is played to a draw. Black must be alert for this pitch as it almost wins.

B. 8-11, 6-8, 4-11, 19-15. White wins.

C. 8-11, 10-26, 11-16, 19-15, 16-19, 26-23. White wins.

D. 11-16, 27-23*, 20-27—E, 31-24, 18-27, 21-17, 16-23, 17-19, 27-32, 24-20, 32-27, 29-25 etc. White wins.

E. 18-27, 21-17, 16-23, 17-19, 4-8, 19-23, 27-32, 23-19, 20-27, 31-24, 32-27, 24-20, 8-11, 29-25, 27-31, 25-22, 31-26, 22-18, 26-22, 19-15, 12-16, 15-8, 22-15, 20-11. White wins.

Game 23

9-13, 23-19, 6-9

Here is a game the Editor played in the New York Masters' Tournament in 1934 with Jesse B. Hanson, noted Internationalist. Though this was early in the three move era, the defense adopted serves as a model for this opening. We believe you will enjoy the notes by Willie Ryan, which are written in his usual breezy style.

Kenneth M. Grover—Black Jesse B. Hanson—White

9-13	1-6	2-6—E	14-17
23-19	28-24	24-20	23-18
6-9—A	8-11	14-17—E	15-19
19-15—B	15-8	21-14	18-14
10-19	4-11	10-17	19-24
24-15	22-18	31-26—F	22-18
11-18	6-10	6-10—G	24-27
22-15	29-25	20-16	26-23
7-11—C	9-14	12-19	27-31
26-22	18-9	23-16	23-19
11-18	5-14	17-21*	31-27
22-15	27-23	25-22—H	19-15
3-7	11-15	10-14	27-24—I
25-22	32-27—D	27-23	Drawn

A. A beautiful three mover with White having a strong game on all variations, though Black's formation is wholly tenable.

B. This early center bust is favored by the masters as being White's strongest attack. Rubin scored with it on Ray Gould in the 8th National Tourney. The same position arises 9-13, 23-18, 6-9, 18-15—same. Another powerful move in lieu of 19-15 is 22-18, while a third alternative is 27-23. All are good.

C. The real key to the Black defense and marks a decided improvement on previous analysis and practice where 1-6 was played and White gets in his 25-22. This immediate pressure removes the strong "apex" piece from White's formation. I played 1-6 on Reynolds in the 8th National Tourney, but ultimately discovered its weakness. Later I found this move (7-11) and showed it to Grover who uses it here in good style! Black's draw after 1-6 goes like this: 1-6, 25-22, 7-11, 29-25, 11-18, 22-15, 3-7, 28-24,

7-11, 26-22, 11-18, 22-15, 8-11* (13-17, 21-14, 9-18, loses by 31-26* in reply), 15-8, 4-11, 25-22, 6-10, 27-23, 9-14, 31-26, 2-7* will draw, but is treacherous—Ryan vs. Reynolds.

D. A surprise move by Hanson which carries all the sting of White's superior position. A splendidly selected move. Post mortem efforts failed to show a better move than the one Hanson took. 31-26 is effectively throttled by 7-11* in reply, while 31-27 lets Black through easily by 15-18, 30-26, 7-11, 26-22, 11-15, 24-20, 2-7, 23-19 draws, but on the run—and how!

E. A masterly combination by Grover which forms the proper sequence to Black's draw. Any other procedure would spell disaster.

F. The strongest move. 27-24 is met by the peculiar 6-9.

G. This move draws, but is altogether too wobbly for sound comfort. Grover here missed his chance to force a clean cut draw, which I saw at the time the game was going on. See diagram:

Black to Play and Draw

Continue from diagram: 7-11, 25-22, 17-21*!, 27-24, 21-25*!, 30-21, 12-16, 21-17, 6-9, 23-18, 16-19, 17-14, 19-28, 14-5, 13-17. Drawn—Clear as a bell.

H. A wave of murmurs arose from the large throng of spectators when Hanson made this one. All had expected Jesse to go for a king by 16-12 and it certainly was his best move. Meanwhile, on another board in the far corner of the room, New York's well known and celebrated "kibitzers" had been busy and were whispering around that Hanson missed a chance to tie the score with Grover. Curious to see their play, I joined the kibitzers' table with the following conclusions resulting. Continue from Note H: 16-12, 7-11*, 12-8, 11-16, 8-3, 10-14*, 3-7, 16-20* (not 15-19, then 27-23 and the kibitzers win!), 26-23, 15-18*, 23-19, 14-17, 7-10 . . . and here the kibitzers gave up the position as hopeless for Black. But continue: 18-23*!, 27-18, 17-22, 18-14, 22-29, 10-15, 13-17, 19-16, 20-24, 15-19, 24-27, 14-9, 27-31. Drawn. Can you beat it?

I. The game continued a few more moves when a draw was agreed on. This was one of the most closely contested games in the tourney.

Game 24

9-14, 22-18, 11-16

The following game was contested between the finalists of the 1938 New York Masters' Tournament.

Tommie Wiswell—Black Harold Freyer—White

9-14	18-9	16-20—D	17-14
22-18	6-13	15-11—E	22-25
11-16	23-18—A	2-6—F	9-5
18-9	16-23	32-28	25-30
5-14	26-19	20-24—F	14-10
24-19	10-15	22-17	30-25
8-11	19-10	13-22	11-7
25-22	7-23	26-17	25-22
11-15	27-18	6-9—F	7-2
29-25	12-16	17-13	22-18
15-24	25-22	9-14—F	2-6*—G
28-19	16-19	13-9	Drawn
4-8	30-26	14-18	By
22-18	11-16—B	21-17	Perpetual
8-11	18-15—C	18-22	Check

Notes by Harold Freyer

A. 25-22, 2-6, 23-18, 16-23, 26-19, 11-16, 27-23, 7-11, 30-26, 6-9, 32-28, 1-5, 22-17, 13-22, 26-17, 9-14, 18-9, 5-14, 17-13, 11-15, 13-9, 15-24, 28-19, 3-7, 9-6, 7-11, 6-1, 11-15, 1-6, 15-24, 6-15, 24-27. Drawn—Ryan vs. Rubin, First N. C. A. Championship, and Freyer vs. Herman.

B. Published play goes 3-7. This 11-16 also appears sound for a draw. It is forceful and devoid of complications.

C. White hasn't much choice here. 32-28 allows 16-20, 31-27, 3-8 and gives Black a strong game, but White draws by 18-15, 2-7, 27-23*, 8-12, 23-16, 12-19, 22-18, 20-24, 15-11, 7-16, 26-23, 19-26, 28-12. Drawn.

White can also play 18-14, 3-7 and has nothing better than a draw by 14-10, 7-14, 22-17, 13-22, 26-10, 19-23, 21-17, 16-20, 17-13, 20-24, 13-9, 1-5, 32-28, 5-14, 28-19, 14-18, 19-15. Drawn—a neat counterpart position.

D. This move is very forceful.

E. 22-18 allows 3-7, 32-28 also allows 3-7 and White's advantage is dissipated. I noticed that 2-6 in reply to 15-11 checked 22-18, but I had no better than text.

F. With these moves Mr. Wiswell forces a very novel position which gets him a well-earned draw.

G. If this game is sound, it may be the standard draw line for black against 23-18, as the White moves are all forced, or else White has no advantage. This game was finely contested by Mr. Wiswell.

Game 25

10-14, 22-17

10-14—A	31-26	4-8—J	30-23
22-17—B	1-6	32-28	6-9
7-10—1, C	25-22	8-11—J	13-6
17-13	18-25	24-19	2-9
3-7	29-22	15-24	19-15
24-20—F	14-17	28-19	12-16
14-18—G	21-14	11-16—J	15-10
23-14	10-17	20-11	Drawn
9-18	23-18	7-16	G. M. Bonar
26-23	11-15	23-18	vs.
10-14	18-11	16-23	James Ferrie
28-24	8-15	26-19	
6-10	27-23	17-26	

A. Forms the Denny. This opening requires careful play on Black's part because of the number of strong attacks at White's command.

B. Best. This attack gives White many opportunities to gain the upper hand.

C. 14-18 is premature and leads to a delicate situation for Black. A New York clique of experts including Willie Ryan, Oliver Mauro, William Link, Vincent Connolly, and the Editors recently unearthed the following strong attack at this point: 14-18, 23-14, 9-18, 17-13, 5-9, 21-17, 11-15—D, 26-22 (Mr. Ryan's suggestion), 12-16, 17-14, 1-5, 22-17, 18-22—E, 25-11, 8-15 (not 9-18 because 24-19 and White wins), 30-26, 9-18, 27-23, 18-27, 32-23, 15-19, 24-15, 4-8 and Black can draw with care.

D. 12-16 is rather shaky because of 25-21, 18-22, 27-23, 16-20, 32-27. Walter Hallman.

E. If 18-23, 27-11, 8-15, 24-19, 16-23, 31-26, 9-18, 26-1. White wins.

F. This side move is confining.

G. Though 11-16 may be more restrictive, it leads to a weak ending for Black. 11-16, 20-11, 8-15, 28-24, 4-8, 23-18—H, 15-22, 26-17 (still confining Black), 14-18, 24-19, 7-11, 17-14, 10-17, 21-14, 11-15, 19-10, 6-15, 13-6, 1-17, 25-22, 17-26, 30-14, 15-18, 14-10 (better than 29-25, 2-6 the usual continuation here), 18-22 (only move), 32-28, 5-9, 10-6, 9-14, 6-1, 14-17, 1-5, 17-21, 27-23, and Black is left with a tough assignment.

H. White can also play 23-19 and 15-18 will draw, but 8-11 loses by 26-22. (See Mid Game Structures—The Whip.)

J. Keeping White at bay. If Black should play 17-21 here instead of text, he would not only release this grip but also greatly reduce the value of this man in any future development of the game.

Variation 1

6-10, 17-13, 1-6 runs into an exciting game between Willie Ryan (Black) and the writer that was played at the 9th National Tourney at Martins Ferry, Ohio. Our game came up from 9-14, 22-17, 5-9, 17-13, 1-5 and continued:

25-22	10-17	26-22—B	22-26
14-17	13-9	17-26	3-7—C
21-14	5-14	31-22	4-8
9-25	23-19	12-16	7-3
29-22	15-24—A	22-17	8-12
10-15	28-19	15-18	3-7
22-17	16-23	17-14	12-16
6-10	27-9	16-19	7-11
24-20	2-6—A	14-10	16-20
11-16	9-2	19-23	Drawn
20-11	3-7—A	10-7	
7-16	2-11	18-22	
17-14	8-15	7-3	

A. Only move to draw.

B. After the game we were both surprised to learn that A. J. Heffner had published play to this point, varying with 32-28.

C. 32-27, 23-32, 30-23, was suggested for a try at First Position. 32-27, 23-18, 27-23, 18-14, 23-18, 14-9, 18-14, 9-5, 14-9, 5-1, 9-5. Draws.

Game 26

10-15, 21-17, 11-16

Kenneth M. Grover—Black Everett Fuller—White

10-15—L	26-17	1-6	18-9
21-17—A	16-20	25-21	5-14
11-16—A	29-25	6-9	17-13
22-18	4-8	26-22—H	2-6
15-22	24-19	8-11	19-15—J
25-18	11-16	28-24	10-26
8-11	17-14—B	7-10	24-19
30-25	6-10	14-7	16-23
9-13	31-26—C	3-10	27-2—K
25-21	10-17	22-17	Drawn
13-22	21-14	9-14	

A. This opening favors White in most of the variations and has the added advantage of allowing White the freedom to vary at many stages to broaden the scope of the play.

B. White is building up a strong center, confining Black to the side of board. The setting now has the characteristics of a typical Dyke formation. This pattern consists of having a man stationed on square 14 (when you have the White side) plus having occupancy or control of the squares 18, 19, 23, 26, 27, 31, and 32. (Or squares 1, 2, 6, 7, 10, 14, 15 occupied or controlled if you have Blacks, plus a piece on square 19.) We have arrived at a Dyke formation indirectly.

C. Places the game on a one way route. White could complicate the position and have scoring chances with 18-15, 10-17, 21-14, 1-6—D, 28-24, 7-10—E, 14-17, 3-10, 31-26, 5-9, 26-22, 9-14, 22-18, 14-7, 25-21, 17-22, 18-14, 10-17, 21-14, 6-10. Drawn—Everett Fuller.

D. Mr. Fuller pointed out the win if 7-11 is made: 7-11, 15-10, 11-15, 25-22—F, 15-24, 28-19, 2-6—G, 27-24, 20-27, 31-24, 6-15, 19-10, 16-20, 32-27, 8-11, 22-18, 11-16, 24-19, 3-8, 18-15. White wins.

E. This releases any threat for a White win. The move 6-9 appears uninviting because of 15-11, 8-15, 19-10, 9-18, 23-14.

F. 28-24 loses by 15-18, 31-26, 5-9, 14-5, 8-11, 23-14, 16-30. Black wins.

G. White also wins if 8-11, 22-18, 2-6, 19-15, 3-8, 31-26, 6-9, 26-22, 9-13, 32-28.

H. 28-24 calls for 7-10, 14-7, 3-10 to break the grip, followed by 26-22, 8-11, running back into the trunk. Mr. Fuller was moving rapidly, seeing his forced draw at Note J.

J. After the game Mr. Fuller remarked that he was playing for this climax from 31-26 (Note C).

K. A game appearing in the 9th American Tourney Book.

L. Forms the Kelso.

Game 27

11-16, 22-18, 16-19

Kenneth M. Grover—Black — Ray Gould—White

11-16—D	4-8	9-13	10-17
22-18	27-24	25-21	21-14
16-19—A	7-10	13-22	1-6
24-15	24-15	26-17	27-24
10-19	10-19	16-20	20-27
23-16	21-17	31-27	32-16
12-19	11-16	8-11	11-20
25-22	17-14	17-13	26-23
8-11	2-7—B	6-10	6-10
29-25	22-17—C	30-26	Drawn

A. This Dyke formation favors White. Black's obstacle is the man on 18. This game was played in the 9th U. S. Championship. Ray Gould, holder of several New England championships, and prize winner in many American tournies, piloted the White pieces.

B. Forced. 3-7 loses by 14-10, 7-23, 28-24, 19-28, 26-3. White wins.

C. A strong move that maintains White's superior position.

D. Forms the Bristol.

Game 28

11-16, 23-18, 8-11

After Walter Hallman and I had divided third and fourth prizes at the 9th American Tournament, The Miami Checker Club, under the sponsorship of Mr. O. J. Tanner, arranged a 20 game match between us. This is the 17th game of the match at which stage Mr. Hallman needed a win to tie the score. However, I managed to escape defeat in the remaining games.

Kenneth M. Grover—Black Walter Hallman—White

11-16	28-19	12-16	5-1
23-18	7-11—C	32-28—E	10-15
8-11—A	22-18—2	2-7	1-10
18-14—B	10-15	14-9—F	19-24
9-18	19-10	15-19	10-19
22-8	6-22	31-26	24-31
4-11	30-26	3-8	19-15
25-22—1	5-9—D	25-22	31-27
16-20	26-17	8-12	15-18
26-23	9-13	9-5	27-31
11-15	17-14	7-10	18-15
24-19	11-15	21-17—G	31-27—J
15-24	29-25	1-6—H	Drawn

A. A three mover giving White a slight edge.

B. Though considered strong, I believe the game fairly even. White has not much more than the choice of lines on most of the variations.

C. The position also arises from **10-15, 23-18, 12-16, 26-23, 16-20, 24-19, 15-24, 28-19, 8-12, 18-14, 9-18, 22-8, 4-11, 25-22, 7-10.** (Kear's.)

D. I prefer this move to 11-15, as given between R. T. Ward and L. Collingwood. The game, as given in Kear's, was formed from the 10-15, 23-18, 12-16 opening.

Black can now work out a theme for the development of his position. We get partial control of White's single corner by going 5-9, then 9-13. Our next step would be to take the center and start cramping White's double corner. This we do by placing pieces on 15 and 16 from 11 and 12 and later using the men on 2 and 3 for fortification, if needed, viz.: 2-7, 3-8, etc. Later 15-19 starts to force the issue.

E. If White goes 14-10, Black replies 15-19, 23-18, and 19-23!! Black wins. Also, if 14-9 instead of 14-10, go 2-7 and we would run into the trunk, but Black could choose 3-7 and White would need a microscope to find the draw, if any.

F. Now if 25-22, 15-19 runs into the trunk, but had I taken the three for three, which looks like a fancy draw, it would have been curtains. Hallman showed me this win right after the game: 16-19, 23-16, 7-11, 16-7, 2-26, 31-22, 1-6, 27-23, 6-10, 23-18, 15-19, 18-15, 10-14, 15-10, 20-24, 10-6, 24-27, 6-1, 27-31, 1-5. White wins. The chances are, if Hallman had played 25-22, I would have replied 15-19, inasmuch as most of my ideas seemed to end up as the game was actually played.

G. Not 22-18, because 20-24. Black wins.

H. The move that clears up the game for Black.

J. An interesting original game with forced play for both sides.

Variation 1

The following is Willie Ryan's preference at this point:

24-20	17-13	8-4	11-18
16-19	11-16*	6-10	10-14
25-22	20-11	31-27	18-9
11-15	7-16	12-16	5-14
27-24	24-20	4-8	13-9
5-9	14-18	16-20	25-22
22-17	20-11	26-23	9-5
9-14	18-23	19-26	22-26
29-25	27-18	30-23	23-19
3-8	15-29	29-25	14-18
32-27	11-8	8-11	Drawn
8-11	10-15	1-5	

Variation 2

Edwin F. Hunt played 30-26 against Asa Long in their World's Championship match. The game continued:

30-26	21-17	13-9	10-14
11-15	14-21	14-17	21-25
19-16	29-25	9-6	32-28
12-19	21-30	17-22	25-30
23-16	16-12	6-2	28-24
2-7	30-23	10-14	20-27
22-17	27-2	2-6	31-24
5-9	1-5	14-17	Drawn
17-13	2-9	6-10	
9-14	5-14	17-21	

Game 29

11-16, 24-19, 16-20

Willie Ryan—Black Kenneth M. Grover—White

11-16	4-8	6-24	3-10
24-19—A	32-27	22-17—G	14-7
16-20—A	8-11	13-22	23-18
22-17	19-15	26-17	7-3
8-11	11-16	12-16	16-20
17-14—B	15-10—D	8-4	4-8
10-17	16-19—E	24-28	24-27
21-14	30-26	27-23	31-24
9-18	9-13	28-32	20-27
23-14	18-15	23-18	3-7
11-16	2-6	20-24	5-9
27-23—C	25-22	18-15—H	17-14
6-9	19-24—F	32-27	Drawn
23-18	28-19	15-10	
16-23	7-11	27-23	
26-19	15-8	10-7—J	

A. White has a slight edge but the opportunities for both to score are many. The games arising from this opening can easily change into lines of play starting from a different order of moves. Mr. Ryan and the writer played the above game in the semi-finals of the 9th Tourney.

B. Strives for a Dyke formation, but by going 25-22, 9-14, 22-18, 4-8, 18-9, 5-14 we would have a Pioneer formation, coming from 9-14, 22-17, and many other openings.

C. White has other moves at his disposal, 25-21, 25-22, and 26-23. The text varies from published play forcing Willie and me into unexplored grounds.

D. Complicating the position with an offer of playing a gambit if necessary. Black can steal the man on 10 by moving 7-11, 25-21, 2-6, 10-7, 3-17, 21-14, 9-13, 29-25, 13-17, 25-22, 17-26, 30-23, 6-9, 28-24, 9-13, 24-19, 13-17, 19-15, 17-22, 15-8, 16-19. Drawn.

I think my readers will find it interesting if I pause here and (with the aid of my associate, Mr. Wiswell) make a few remarks regarding the playing style of some of the leading American experts. Each of the outstanding masters has certain characteristics that distinguish him from his fellow players and are often the real secrets of his success.

For example, Asa Long, the World's Champion, usually adopts solid book lines that he has previously analyzed thoroughly. He handles his endings superbly and often scores by improving on published play at this stage of the game.

Willie Ryan, on the other hand, is more apt to adopt unorthodox lines of play, always assuring himself of their soundness before using them in tournament or match play. For this reason his games tend to be more spectacular and colorful and at the same time are extremely troublesome because his opponents never know what to expect.

Walter Hallman and Nathan Rubin are players of an entirely different type. They are known as "safe" players. Both have such an extensive knowledge of published play on two move and three move restriction that they are in a class by themselves in this respect. While both are fine crossboard performers, Long and Ryan probably have a slight edge on them.

Edwin F. Hunt, former U. S. Champion, is a fine all around player of the same school as Rubin and Hallman. There is no player anywhere more gentlemanly or sportsmanlike in his playing conduct than this wizard of the Southland.

Young Harold Freyer of New York does not yet possess the knowledge and experience of these famous masters but he more than compensates for this by his conscientiousness and hard working determination. He usually takes his full time in moving and seldom is guilty of snap judgment.

Newell W. Banks has a dashing style all his own and in his prime was without peer as a crossboard player. Another great crossboard performer, much along the same lines, is Louis C. Ginsberg of Brooklyn, N. Y.

It is Ginsberg who has probably served more to influence my style of play and act as a model for me than any other player, though L. T. deBearn also inspired me with his brilliant style. DeBearn's ability immediately to grasp the potentialities and possibilities of a position impressed me immensely. Since the advent of 3 move, Ryan has given me the polish I have needed to climb to the top.

I have a tendency to study many games only to a key point and from there rely upon my ability to carry me through. Like Ginsberg, I make the formations of games the basis of my study and do not keep an extensive manuscript like the majority of outstanding players. I am not averse to departing from the beaten path and if my opponent happens to do likewise I am always ready to gamble a bit in an attempt to score. "Nothing ventured, nothing gained" has been my motto and though it has sometimes proved a dangerous one to follow, I think it accounts more than anything else for whatever successes I have achieved in the checker world.

E. Ryan does not want the piece but offers me a gambit. If 27-24, 20-27, 31-15, 9-13 and with 5-9 threatened White can resign.

F. Black is trying for an ending.

G. Preparations must be made to break the bridge (pieces on 1 and 3 form the bridge).

H. Avoiding 14-10, 3-8, 4-27, 32-7 wins for Black.

J. Breaking the bridge insures the draw.

Game 30

12-16, 24-20, 8-12

12-16—A	5-14	12-19	16-19
24-20—B	22-17	26-23	23-16
8-12—C	6-10	19-26	28-32
28-24	17-13	30-23	16-12
3-8	1-6	11-16	32-27
22-18	29-25	20-11	12-8
16-19	8-12—D	7-16	27-24
24-15	25-22	32-28	8-3
10-19	11-15	15-19	24-19
23-16	22-17	31-26	22-18
12-19	4-8	2-7	14-23
25-22	27-23	28-24	17-14
9-14	8-11	19-28	Drawn
18-9	23-16	26-22	Published Play

A. This single move forms the Dundee and vies with the Denny (10-14) as being the weakest debut for Black next to the Edinburgh (9-13).

B. Best, for with this move White gains an immediate positional advantage. Note how Black's entire single corner is now cramped.

C. If 10-15 at this point, White can secure a powerful game by 22-18, 15-22, 25-18, 8-12, 28-24, 6-10 (or 7-10), 18-14, 10-17, 21-14, 9-18, 23-14.

D. Black keeps out of trouble with this move. In a match game with Walter Hallman I played 11-16 at this stage and barely succeeded in getting a hair line draw. This is how the Gary master put me into a tight spot: 11-16, 20-11, 8-15, 25-22, 4-8, 21-17—E, 14-21, 30-25, 21-30, 22-17, 30-23, 27-4, 19-23, 4-8, 10-15—F, 17-14, 15-18, 8-3, 7-11, 14-9, 18-22, 3-7, 11-16, 31-27, 2-11, 9-2, 23-26, 2-7, 26-30, 27-24, 30-26, 24-20 which ultimately draws. White seems to have a deadly grip on the pieces on 11 and 16 but Black has a problem draw as analyzed by Chris Nelson and the late Sam Gonotsky. This is a historic position on which a multitude of play has been published in the various checker columns and periodicals. After several years of pro and con, regarding Black's drawing chances, the critics concluded that the position was tenable. Nevertheless, the line is usually shunned by the good players. We think you will enjoy going over the position and exploring the many ramifications involved. The amount of play that could be unearthed would fill many pages of a book and for that reason we leave the position for your consideration at this stage. Do you agree with the conclusions of the critics?

E. Published play in numerous textbooks erroneously stars 22-18 to win at this point. In reality the position is an easy draw with Black having some winning chances on certain variations. In a practice game with my sparring partner, Tommy Wiswell, just before the 9th National Tourney, we arrived at this position. But first let us diagram it for you:

White (Wiswell) to Play, Black Draw

Our game continued as follows: 22-18, 15-22, 26-17, 7-11, 27-23, 19-26, 30-23, 11-15, 31-27, 8-11, 27-24, 15-18, 23-19, 18-23, 19-15, 11-18, 24-19, 23-27, 32-23, 18-27, 19-15. Drawn.

While there are, of course, other ways for White to play than the above, Black can secure a safe draw regardless. It would seem that numerous authors have noted that 22-18 is starred to win and included it in their manuscript without taking the trouble to investigate the truth of the matter. This is the only explanation we can give for its being in so many textbooks.

F. If 7-11, 8-15, 10-19, 17-14, 6-10, 14-7, 2-11, 13-9, 11-15, 9-6, 15-18, 31-27. White wins.

MID GAME STRUCTURES

Most players, especially those unfamiliar with the study of scientific checkers, are apt to have a great deal of trouble with the mid game. Due to the complicated nature of this phase of the game, it is without a doubt more treacherous than the Opening or End-game. This is especially true as far as the beginner is concerned.

For purposes of study we have divided this chapter into two sections. Each deals with a distinctive phase of the mid game to which the reader must pay particular attention. These sections are:

1. Pitfalls, or traps and shots.
2. Familiar Landings and Transpositions.

First we deal with the many traps and shots that dot the mid-game like so many mines laid in warring waters. Until the student becomes familiar with these numerous danger spots he will have little or no chance at all of surviving the mid game.

Next we deal with the subject of Familiar Landings. This subject has been either entirely neglected or just barely alluded to in most textbooks on checkers, despite the fact that familiar landings and the various ways in which they can be reached, constitute a very important part of every expert's "bag of tricks." We have illustrated some of the more important patterns that are formed over and over again in the mid game. For two very good reasons we include many losing formations as well as some that lead to sound draws. First, so that you will be able to avoid these untenable situations yourself, and secondly so that you will be able to score once your unsuspecting opponent plays into them.

The important thing to remember about this latter phase of the mid game (Familiar Landings) is the fact that these patterns or positions can be arrived at in innumerable ways. Sometimes these positions are exact replicas while again the identical themes may be involved although there will be a slight difference in the arrangement of pieces. The successful checker strategist must understand and be able to employ this art of transposition. Once you have mastered this very valuable little trick it will be possible for you to lure your opponents into many traps *he has studied* as well as those he is unfamiliar with. The point is that your less experienced adversary being unacquainted with the art of transposition will not recognize the old traps you have laid for him in their new guise. The beginner is not the only one who can be caught with this subtle little art. We cite the following amusing incident to prove our point. First let us show you one of the oldest traps known in the game of checkers. It usually comes up as follows: 11-16, 23-18, 16-20, 24-19, and now 10-14 will draw, but 8-11 loses and forms the position on the diagram:

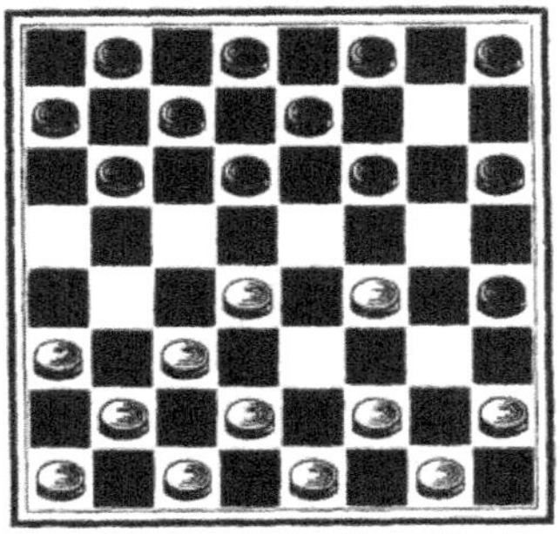

White to Play and Win

Now every expert knows that 19-15, 10-19, 18-14, 9-18, 22-8, 4-11, 27-24, 20-27, 31-8 will win for White. Note that we said this trap *usually* comes up from the order of moves we have given and it is this run-up that is invariably shown when this trap is illustrated in the various textbooks. In a recent mid-western state tournament two fairly strong players ballotted this three move opening: 12-16, 24-19, 16-20. After White moved 23-18, Black played 8-12 unmindful of the fact that he had blundered into this famous trap by a slightly different order of moves than is generally given.

So you see it was possible for this seasoned tournament player to stumble into a well known loss on his third move simply because he did not appreciate the fact that he had arrived at a common danger spot by a new route. The memory of this expert's tragedy in the opening may make the reader aware of the far more complicated dangers of the same type, that lurk all through the midgame, and consequently instil in him a sense of care and watchfulness.

Let us proceed with the first phase of our study of the mid game

Diagram 1

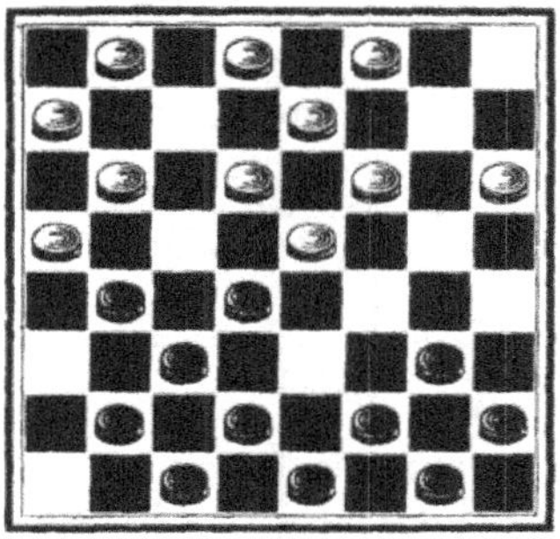

Black to Play and Win

Diagram 2

Black to Play and Win

The trap in diagram 1 comes up as follows: 11-15, 22-18, 15-22, 25-18, 8-11, 29-25, 4-8, 24-20, 10-15, 25-22, 12-16 (setting the trap), and now 21-17 is the draw move, but 27-24 (forms diagrammed position) and 28-24 both look safe enough to the player who doesn't look below the surface. Both moves lose as follows: 16-19, 23-16, 15-19, 24-15, 9-14, 18-9, 11-25 and Black has a winning formation. This loss is called the "Goosewalk."

A similar type of trap that comes up a bit earlier in the Kelso is shown in diagram 2. It arises as follows: 10-15, 22-18, 15-22, 25-18, 6-10, 29-25, 10-15 (setting the trap), now 18-14 and 26-22 draw, but 25-22 (forms diagrammed position) the most natural looking move goes out by 15-19, 24-15, 9-14, 18-9, 11-25 and Black wins.

Diagram 3

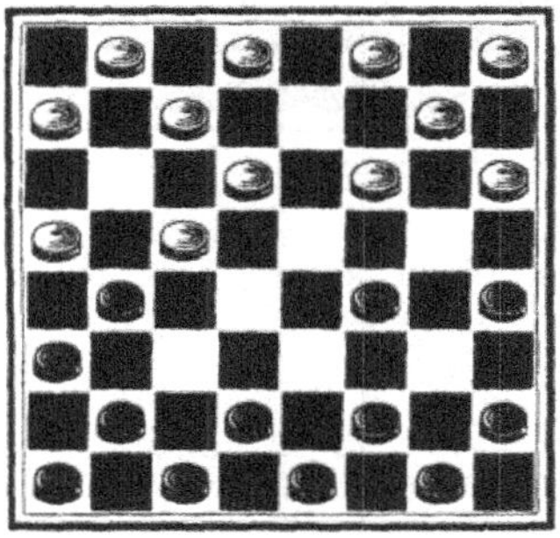

Black to Play and Win

Diagram 4

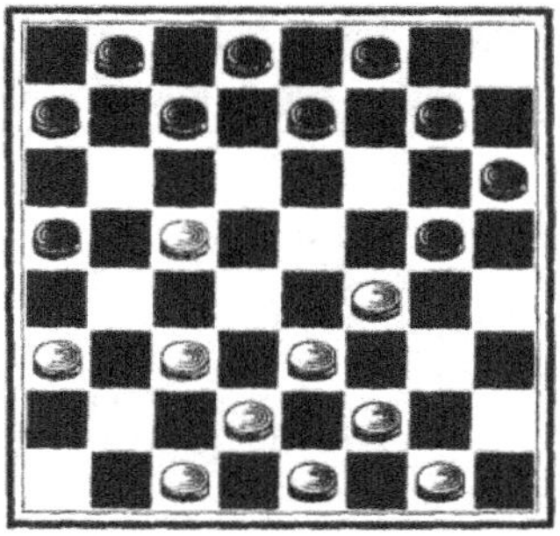

White to Play and Win

Diagram 3: 10-14, 23-19, 11-16, 26-23, 9-13, 24-20 (loses and forms the diagrammed position. 22-17 draws), 14-17, 21-14, 6-10, 20-11, 10-26, 31-22, 8-31. Black wins.

Diagram 4: Can come up numerous ways. Here are a few illustrations:

1. 11-15, 22-18, 15-22, 25-18, 8-11, 29-25, 10-15, 25-22, 4-8, 24-19, 15-24, 28-19, 9-13, 18-14, 11-16 (loses and forms diagrammed position. 6-9 draws).
2. 11-15, 24-20, 8-11, 23-18, 15-19, 18-14, 9-18, 22-8, 4-11, 25-22, 5-9, 29-25, 9-14, 22-17 forms diagram, colors reversed.
3. 11-15, 23-18, 8-11, 24-20, 15-19, 18-14, 9-18, 22-8, 4-11, 21-17, 5-9, 25-21, 9-14, 29-25 forms diagram, colors reversed.
4. 10-15, 22-17, 9-13, 17-14, 15-19, 24-15, 11-18, 25-22, 18-25, 29-22, 8-11, 28-24, 4-8, 24-19, 11-16 forms diagram.

The win is as follows (from illustration 1. Of course the idea is the same in each of the following examples, though the colors may be reversed), 14-10, 7-14, 22-17, 13-22, 26-10, 6-24, 27-4. White wins.

Diagram 5

White to Play and Win

Diagram 6

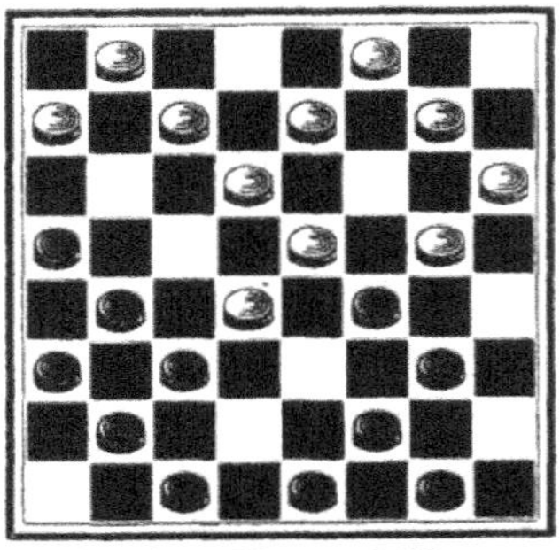

Black to Play and Win

Diagram 5: (The Brooklyn Stroke) 11-15, 22-18, 15-22, 25-18, 12-16, 29-25, 9-13, 18-14, 10-17, 21-14, 16-20, 23-18, 6-10, 25-21, 10-17, 21-14, 1-6, 26-23, 13-17, 31-26, 8-11, 24-19, 4-8, 28-24, 8-12, 19-15, 3-8, 23-19, 11-16, 26-22, 17-26, 30-23, 7-10 (loses and forms diagram. 6-10 and 7-11 draw). White wins as follows: 14-7, 2-11, 18-14, 11-18, 14-10, 6-15, 23-14, 16-23, 27-4. White wins.

Diagram 6: 9-14, 22-18, 5-9, 25-22, 11-16, 24-19, 8-11, 29-25 (loses, 22-17 draws. See Game 14), 4-8, 27-24, 16-20, 31-27, 11-16.

19-15, 10-19, 24-15, 7-11, 22-17 (forms diagrammed position). Here is how we do it. 16-19, 17-10 (23-7, 3-19, 17-10, 6-31. Black wins), 19-24, 28-19, 9-14, 18-9, 11-18, 23-14, 6-31, 26-22, 12-16 etc. Black wins.

Diagram 7

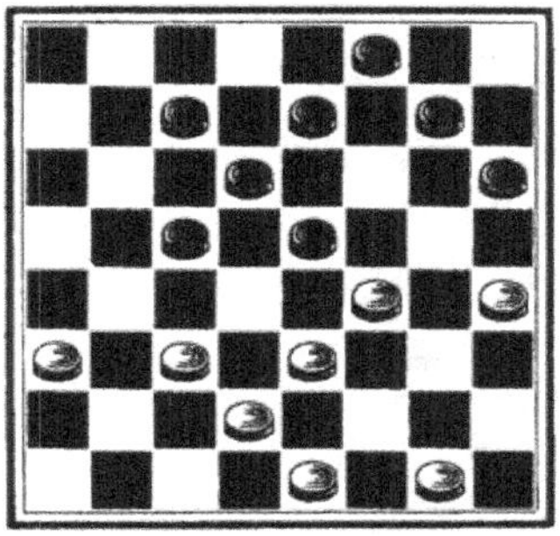

White to Play and Win

Diagram 8

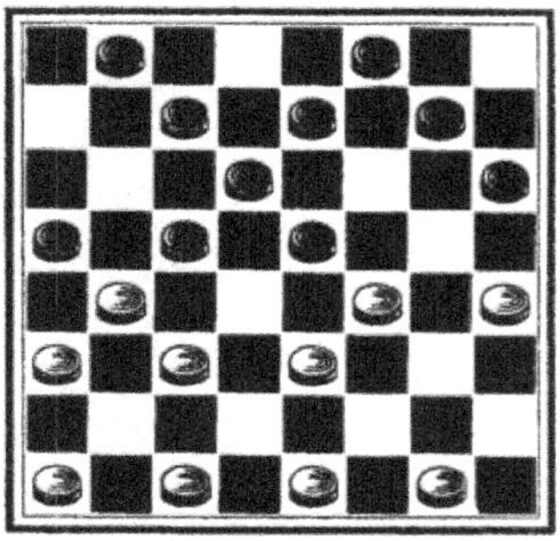

White to Play and Win

Diagram 7: 11-15, 23-18, 8-11, 27-23, 4-8, 23-19, 9-13 (loses. 9-14 or 10-14 draws. See Game 1–Game 3), 26-23, 6-9, 30-26, 9-14, 18-9, 5-14, 22-17 (32-27 has also been given to win), 13-22, 25-9, 1-5, 29-25, 5-14, 25-22, 2-6, 24-20, 15-24, 28-19, 11-15 (forms diagram), 20-16 (the tempo move that cinches the win), 15-24, 22-18, 12-19, 18-2. White wins.

Diagram 8: 11-15, 23-19, 8-11, 22-17, 4-8, 25-22, 9-13, 27-23, 6-9, 23-18, 9-14, 18-9, 5-14, 26-23, 2-6 (1-6 is best), 24-20, 15-24, 28-19, 11-15 (forms diagrammed position. 6-9 draws narrowly), 20-16, 15-24, 22-18, 12-26, 18-2, 13-22, 2-4. White wins.

FAMILIAR LANDINGS

It is extremely difficult, even for the seasoned player, to avoid the many pitfalls of the mid game. While it is a comparatively easy matter to drift into an untenable formation at this stage of the game, it is practically impossible to extricate yourself once you are caught.

Here is a loss that arises from numerous openings, some times under a slightly different arrangement of the pieces:

Illustration 1

10-14, 24-20, 11-16, 20-11, 8-15, 28-24, 6-10, 22-17, 4-8, 17-13, 1-6, 23-19, 8-11—A. Black's last move is the loser and forms the diagram. 15-18 draws as shown in Note A.

The Whip

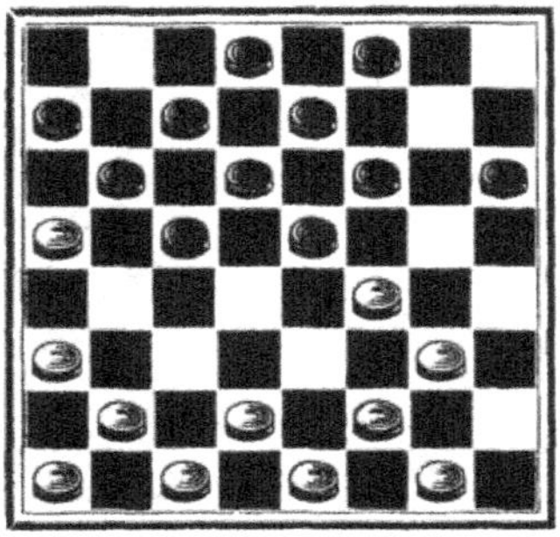

White to Play and Win

White now cinches the win with 26-22 (a real "binder"). Black has four playable moves and they all lose:

1. If 3-8, 22-17, 15-18, 19-15 White wins.
2. If 11-16, 24-20, 15-24, 20-11, 7-16, 27-11 White wins.
3. If 14-18, 24-20, 15-24, 22-8 White wins.
4. If 14-17, 21-14, 9-18, 24-20 White wins.

A. 15-18 is the move that keeps Black out of danger as it prevents the immediate tie-up permitted by 8-11. This 15-18 was adopted by Mr. Grover in a game with Asa Long at the 9th American Championship tournament in 1937 with the following result: 15-18, 26-23, 8-11, 24-20, 11-15, 32-28, 15-24, 28-19, 3-8, 30-26, 14-17, 21-14, 10-17, 23-14, 9-18, 26-22, 17-26, 31-15, 7-11, 25-22, 11-25, 29-22, 6-10, 27-23, 8-11, 23-18, 2-6, 22-17, 5-9, 17-14, 10-17, 19-15, 9-14. Drawn.

Here are still more games containing the same idea, although the arrangement of the pieces is slightly different in most of them:

Illustration 2

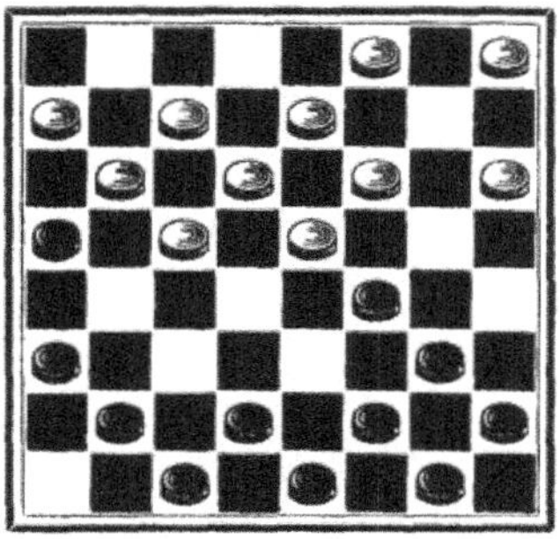

Black to Play and Win
7-11 is the move that does the trick.

Illustration 3

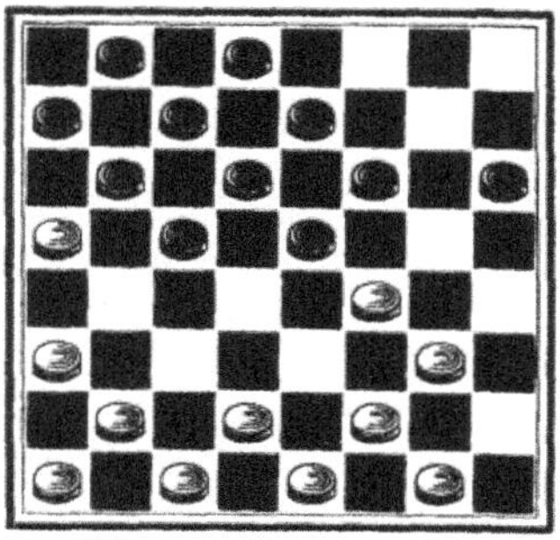

White to Play and Win
By this time you are no doubt well enough acquainted with this formation to pick out the winning move at once—26-22. White wins.

Illustration 2: 11-15, 24-19, 15-24, 28-19, 8-11, 22-18, 11-16, 25-22, 10-14, 27-24, 16-20, 31-27, 4-8, 32-28 (29-25 draws) forms diagram.

Illustration 3: 10-14, 22-17, 7-10, 17-13, 3-7, 24-20, 11-16, 20-11, 8-15, 28-24, 4-8, 23-19, 8-11 (15-18 draws) forms diagram. See Game 25.

Illustrations four and five are identical positions brought up from different openings. Both are typical examples of the formation discussed in this lesson.

Illustration 4

11-15, 23-19, 8-11, 27-23, 11-16, 22-18, 15-22, 25-18, 4-8, 29-25, 16-20, 32-27, 10-14, 25-22 (26-22 draws) forms diagram:

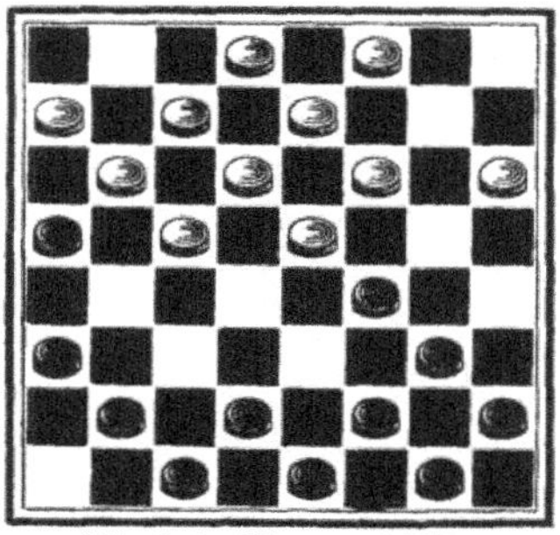

Black to Play and Win
(By 7-11)

Illustration 5

11-15, 22-18, 15-22, 25-18, 12-16, 29-25, 10-14, 24-19, 16-20, 28-24, 8-12, 32-28, 4-8, 25-22 (26-22 draws) forms diagram above. Black wins by 7-11.

Illustration 6

As our concluding example of this theme we give the following subtle version: 10-15, 23-19, 6-10, 22-18, 15-22, 25-18, 10-14, 27-23, 11-16, 29-25, 16-20, 32-27, 8-11, 25-22 (19-16 draws) and 4-8. Black wins.

A PIONEER PATTERN

Here is a Pioneer landing that can be reached in numerous ways. It is a practical position that should be part of every player's mid-game manuscript.

Example 1	*Example 2*	*Example 3*	*Example 4*	*Example 5*
9-14	11-16	11-15	10-15	12-16
22-17	24-19	23-18	22-17	22-17
11-16	8-11	9-14	11-16	16-20
24-19	22-18	18-9	24-19	17-13
8-11	4-8	5-14	15-24	11-15
25-22	25-22	22-17	28-19	25-22
11-15	16-20	8-11	16-20	9-14
17-13	22-17	26-23	17-13	24-19
15-24	9-14	11-16	8-11	15-24
28-19	18-9	24-19	25-22	28-19
4-8	5-14	15-24	11-16	8-11
22-18	29-25	28-19	22-18	22-18
8-11	11-15	7-11	7-10	4-8
18-9	25-22	25-22	26-22	18-9
5-14	15-24	16-20	4-8	5-14
29-25	28-19	17-13	29-25	29-25
16-20	8-11	11-16	9-14	8-12
25-22	17-13	22-17	18-9	25-22
11-16	11-16	4-8	5-14	11-16
22-17	22-17	29-25	22-17	22-17
7-11	7-11	8-11	8-11	7-11
26-22—A	26-22	25-22	25-22	26-22
Forms diagram	Same	Same	Same	Same

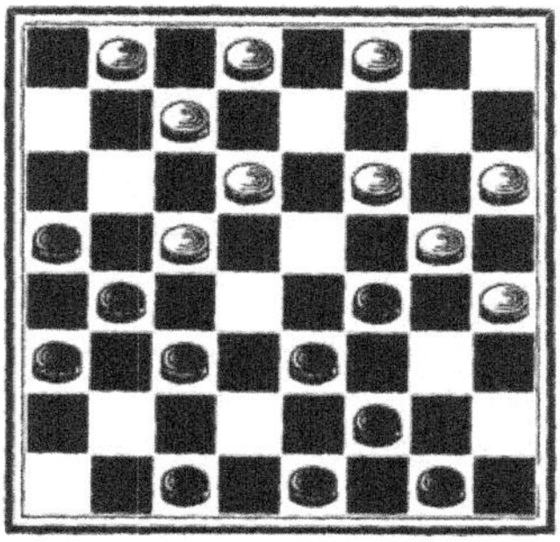

Black to Play

A. For continuation from diagram, see Game 15. Other games running into this familiar landing are as follows:

9-14, 24-19, 11-16, 22-17. Now same as Example 1 at 4th move.

11-15, 24-19, 15-24, 28-19, 8-11, 22-18, 11-16, 25-22, 16-20, 22-17, 4-8, 17-13, 9-14, 18-9, 5-14, 29-25, 8-11. Now same as Example 1 at 17th move.

11-16, 21-17, 9-14, 25-21, 8-11, 24-19. Now same as Example 1 at 6th move.

11-16, 22-17, 9-14, 24-19. Now same as Example 1 at 4th move.

11-16, 24-19, 8-11, 22-17, 9-14. Now same as Example 1 at 5th move.

12-16, 24-19, 8-12, 22-17, 9-14. Now same as Example 1 at 5th move.

12-16, 21-17, 9-14, 25-21, 8-12, 24-19. Now same as Example 1 at 6th move.

There are still other ways in which this position can be reached but these, we think, will suffice to give the reader some idea of the importance of this mid game structure.

A CROSS LANDING

Another important structure you can add to your list of vital formations. You might land in this position from either side of various games.

11-15	11-15	26-23	3-8
23-18	24-20	6-9	15-10
9-14	6-9	32-28—E	21-25
18-11	28-24	10-14	10-6
8-15	9-13	17-10	25-30
22-18	31-27	7-14	6-1
15-22—K	7-11—A	24-19—F	9-14—G
25-9	23-18	15-24	18-9
5-14	14-23	28-19	30-25—J
29-25	27-18	14-17	22-18
4-8	2-7—B, 1	30-26	13-17
25-22	21-17—C	17-21	23-19
8-11	1-6—D	19-15	25-22
27-23			Drawn

A. Forms diagram:

White to Play

Some of the more popular routes leading to this setting are as follows:

9-13, 22-17, 13-22, 25-18, 11-15, 18-11, 8-15, 24-19, 15-24, 28-19, 4-8, 29-25, 8-11, 25-22, 6-9, 27-24, 9-13, 24-20, 5-9, 22-18, 2-6, 26-22 is now the exact position as diagram but with the colors reversed.

9-14, 22-18, 11-15, 18-11, 8-15, 23-18, 15-22, 25-9, 5-14, 29-25, 4-8, 25-22, 8-11, 27-23, 11-15, 24-20, 6-9, 28-24, 9-13, 31-27, 7-11. Same as diagram.

10-15, 23-19, 6-10, 22-18, 15-22, 25-18, 11-15, 18-11, 8-15, 29-25, 4-8, 25-22, 9-13, 27-23, 8-11, 24-20, 15-24, 28-19, 5-9, 22-18, 2-6, 26-22. Same as diagram, colors reversed.

9-14, 24-20, 11-16 (from the 3 move restriction), 20-11, 8-15, 22-18, 15-22, 25-9, 5-14, 29-25, 4-8, 25-22, 8-11, 28-24, 6-9, 24-20, 9-13, 27-24, 11-15, 31-27, 7-11. Here it is again.

Some of the players may know the methods of bringing the diagrammed position from the 11-15, 22-18 opening and the 10-15, 22-18 opening but we have purposely left these out as the positions are brought up with one side making a weak move and the other side not taking advantage of the situation. It is satisfactory to play for certain positions or even traps, but never do so at the expense of weakening your game, because your opponent may not fall into your channels of play.

B. At this stage 2-7 is best, with a narrow draw resulting from 12-16. The other possibilities—10-14, 1-5, 1-6, 2-6, 3-7, and 3-8 all lose for Black. For play on these moves see Variations 1, 2, 3, 4, 5, 6, and 7.

C. If 18-14, 10-17, 21-14, then 3-8 is correct to draw.

D. This move is made to prevent 18-14. 1-5 loses by 18-14, 12-16, 26-23, 3-8, 24-19, 15-24, 22-18, 13-22, 32-28, 10-17, 28-3, 7-10, 3-7. White wins. The popular James Ferrie, one time World's Champion, who played championship caliber checkers when he was over seventy years old, displayed this win.

E. An alternate draw by Teschelelt is 30-25, 12-16, 32-28, 16-19, 23-16, 10-14, 17-10, 7-23, 16-7, 3-10, 24-19, 15-24, 28-19, 23-26, 22-18.

F. A game between Dr. A. Schaefer and J. P. Reed continued: 23-19, 14-23, 19-10, 11-15, 24-19, 15-24, 28-19, 9-14, 22-18, 14-17, 18-15, 17-22, 15-11, 22-26, 10-6, 26-31, 6-1, 23-27, 19-15. Drawn.

G. The play from Note F to this point is by Jesse B. Hanson who had a trap "cooked up" for anyone moving 30-25. Move 30-25, 18-15, 11-27, 1-5, 25-18, 5-32, 13-17—H, 32-27, 17-21, 27-23, 21-25, 23-18, 25-30, 26-22 and White wins shortly.

H. White wins by First Position if 8-11, 32-27, 11-15, 27-31, 13-17, 26-22, 17-26, 31-22.

J. Alex Cameron and Willie Ryan continued with 11-15, 1-6, 15-19 to a draw.

K. For play on 14-23 jump see Game 2.

Variation 1

Black could easily miss the following hard draw as played between Messrs. Whitney and Gilsthorp:

12-16—2	10-14	7-10	26-31
26-23	21-17	8-3	19-16
2-6—A	14-21	10-14	31-26
32-28	23-19	26-23	23-19
6-9	1-5	14-17	9-14
24-19	30-26	3-8	Drawn
15-24	3-7	17-26	
28-12	12-8	8-15	

A. 2-7 would lose by 21-17, 1-5, 18-14, 3-8 as shown in note D of trunk.

Variation 2

Banks played 10-14 in the World's Championship match in 1934, against Long. After the jump 18-9, Banks moved 1-5. Long missed the win when he continued 32-28. James Ricca, a prize winner in the 9th Tourney arrived at this position from the 10-15, 23-19 opening in a game with William Link, a leading New York expert. Link also missed the win. Instead of 32-28 the following will win:

10-14—3	9-14—A, B	7-10	10-19
18-9	32-28—C	22-18	23-7
1-5	3-7	5-9	14-30
9-6*	24-19	30-26	21-5
2-9	15-24	13-17	White
26-23	28-19	19-15	wins

A. 3-7 loses by 21-17 (23-18 also wins as published in Banks-Long match games book), 7-10, 30-25, 9-14, 25-21, 5-9, 32-28, 12-16, 24-19. White wins—Freyer.

B. 3-8 loses by 23-19, 15-18, 22-15, 11-18, 32-27, 18-22, 19-15, 22-25, 24-19, 25-29, 20-16, 29-25, 16-11. White wins.

C. The Long-Banks book offers a win via 21-17, 14-21, 23-19.

Variation 3

This win was found by P. H. Ketchum.

1-5—4, 5	10-6	6-10	9-14
18-14	9-14	26-22	8-12
10-17	6-1	19-23	14-16
21-14	14-18	9-6	12-19
12-16	1-5	3-8	22-18
32-28	18-25	6-9	White
16-19	30-21	23-26	wins
14-10	2-6	21-17	
5-9	5-9	26-30	

Variation 4

W. C. Parrow published this win against 1-6 many years ago. Move 18-14, 10-17, 21-14, 6-10, 14-7, 3-10, 26-23, 2-6, 30-25, 10-14, 25-21, 6-10, 32-28, 12-16, 24-19, 15-24, 28-12, 10-15, 22-18, 15-22, 23-19 and in a few moves the man on 11 is captured.

Variation 5

James Ferrie snared some of his opponents when they tried 2-6 at this point. This win was missed at the 9th Tourney in one of the heats.

2-6—6, 7	6-10—B	1-6	10-15
18-14	14-7	32-28	22-18
10-17	3-10	6-10	15-22
21-14	26-23	24-19	23-19—C
12-16—A	10-14	15-24	White
30-25	25-21	28-12	wins

A. Should 6-10, 14-7, 3-10 be made first, then 26-23 is the move. Proceeding 1-5, 32-28, 5-9, 30-25, 9-14, 25-21, 12-16 and White wins by the same route as above.

B. 6-9, 14-5, 16-19, 32-28, 1-6, 25-21, 6-9, 21-17, 3-8, 5-1, 15-18, 22-15, 11-18, 24-15, 13-31, 20-16, loses for Black—J. Ferrie vs. A. Mauchan.

C. It will be noted that the wins in Variations 4 and 5 pursue the same idea.

Variation 6

P. H. Ketchum defeated P. Matlin when the latter moved 3-7, by 18-14, 10-17, 21-14, 1-5, 32-28, 11-16, 20-11, 7-16, 24-19, 15-24, 28-19, 16-23, 26-19, 2-6, 30-25, 6-9, 14-10, 9-14, 25-21. White wins.

Variation 7

I had 3-8 played against me and won by 26-23, 12-16, 32-28, 8-12, 21-17, 1-5, 18-14, 2-7, 24-19. White wins—Kenneth Grover.

DUNNE'S WIN

All of the following games run into the losing formation known as Dunne's Win. It is comparatively easy to lure a non-book player into this position, but it requires quite a bit of skill to bring the game to a successful conclusion.

Example 1	*Example 2*	*Example 3*
9-14	11-16	12-16
22-17	22-18	22-17
11-16	16-20	8-12
25-22	25-22	25-22
8-11	8-11	9-14
22-18	22-17	22-18
16-20	9-14	16-20
18-9	18-9	18-9
5-14	5-14	5-14
29-25	29-25	29-25
4-8—A	4-8	4-8
Forms diagram	Forms diagram	Forms diagram

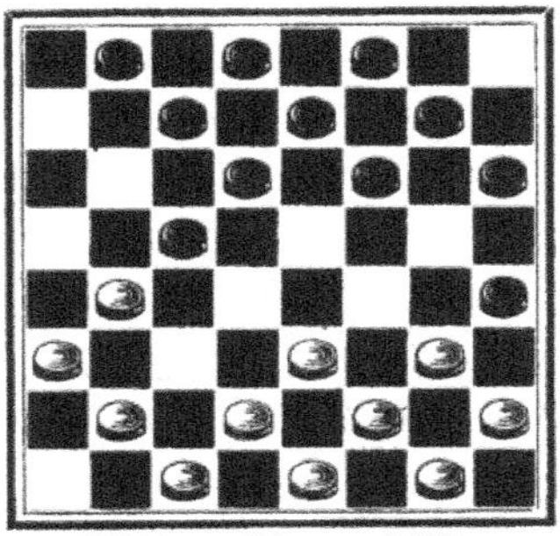

White to Play and Win

A. This and 11-16 (another natural move) both lose and form Dunne's famous win. 11-15 is the move to draw (See Game 15—Variation 1). Take a good look at this position and be sure to keep this 11-15 in mind. It will save you from losing many games. Should you succeed in getting your opponent into this situation here is how to win it:

25-22	28-19	9-5	2-7
11-16	7-11—E	6-10	10-15
24-19	17-13*	5-1	7-16
8-11	11-15	15-19	15-22
22-18	22-17	22-18	16-19
1-5	15-24	19-23	23-26
18-9	23-19	1-6	19-23
5-14—B	16-23	2-9	White
26-22	27-9	13-6	wins
11-15	10-15—F	3-7	(Dunne)
30-25	25-22	6-2	
15-24	24-28	7-11	

B. 6-22, 26-17, 10-14—C, 17-10, 7-14, 31-26*, 3-7, 28-24*, 7-10, 26-22, 11-15, 22-17, 15-18 (If 2-7 then 30-25 wins. However, the student should avoid 17-13 as it loses for White), 30-25, 5-9, 17-13, 2-6, 32-28. White wins.

C. 11-15, 30-25, 15-24, 28-19, 10-14—D, 17-10, 7-14, 25-22, 3-7, 27-24, 20-27, 31-24, 16-20, 22-17, 20-27, 17-3, 27-31, 23-18, 31-26, 18-15, 26-23, 21-17, 26-19, 15-11, 16-7, 3-10, 5-9, 17-13, 12-16, 13-6, 2-9, 32-27. White wins by exchanging off the man now on 16, thereby getting the move.

D. 7-11, 17-14, 10-17, 21-14, 2-6, 25-22, 6-10, 14-7, 3-10, 22-17, 5-9, 17-14, 10-17, 19-15, 11-18, 23-5, 17-22, 32-28, 22-25, 5-1. White wins. The White king finally corners the Black monarch in the single corner.

E. 3-8 is beaten by 19-15, 10-26, 17-1*, 26-30, 1-5, 8-11, 5-9, 7-10, 9-5, 11-15, 5-9, 15-19, 9-5, 19-24, 5-9. White wins. By keeping the man posted on 22 White eventually runs Black out of moves.

F. 3-7, 25-22, 10-15, 9-5, 15-19, 5-1, 6-10, 1-6, 2-9, 13-6, 19-23, 6-2, 7-11, 2-6, 10-15, 6-10, 15-19, 22-18. White wins.

The foregoing three games illustrate the usual way of arriving at this famous position. There are, however, numerous other ways in which White can inveigle Black into the same formation.

Many players who are familiar with the usual continuation leading to Dunne's win have drifted into it via Examples 4 and 5, which follow:

Example 4: 11-16, 23-18, 16-20, 26-23, 8-11, 30-26, 4-8, 22-17, 9-14, 18-9, 5-14—A forming diagram below.

Example 5: 11-16, 22-18, 8-11, 25-22, 16-20, 22-17, 4-8, 30-25, 9-14, 18-9, 5-14 forming diagram.

White to Play and Win

A. The losing jump. 6-22 leads to a safe draw. The White win is as follows: 26-22, 11-16—B, 24-19, 8-11, 22-18, 1-5, 18-9, 5-14—C, 25-22, 11-15, 29-25 and White wins. (Same as trunk solution to Examples 1, 2, and 3 at 11th move.)

B. 1-5, 22-18, 12-16, 18-9, 6-22, 25-18, 10-15, 18-14, 8-12, 29-25, 16-19, 23-16, 12-19, 25-22, 2-6, 31-26, 6-9, 14-10, 7-14, 27-23. White wins.

C. 6-22, 25-18, 10-14, 18-9, 5-14, 29-25, 7-10, 25-22, 11-15, 23-18, 15-24, 18-9, 10-14, 28-19, 16-23, 27-18, 14-23, 22-18, 12-16, 21-17, 16-19, 32-28. White wins.

LESSONS IN THE END-GAME

It has truly been said "The Ending has been the finish of many a player." How often have you played the Opening and Mid Game to perfection, only to falter and lose the game "at the home stretch." It is difficult to overrate the importance of the End-Game. Every first class player has made a systematic and thorough study of this phase of the game.

The various themes elaborated on and illustrated in the following pages, by no means cover all the ideas and maneuvers that crop up in the End-Game but we do believe that they will greatly improve your finishing technique and serve to impress upon you the dangers and delicateness of the End-Game.

We would not advise the reader to go through this section like he were reading an ordinary book. It might be a good idea for you to study one page a day, until you have completed the entire End-Game Section. In this way you will be better able to digest and understand the intricate and interesting plays.

Now let us proceed with Lesson One.

Lesson Number 1

"THE DOUBLE CORNER BLOCK"

Position No. 1
(The Basic Idea)

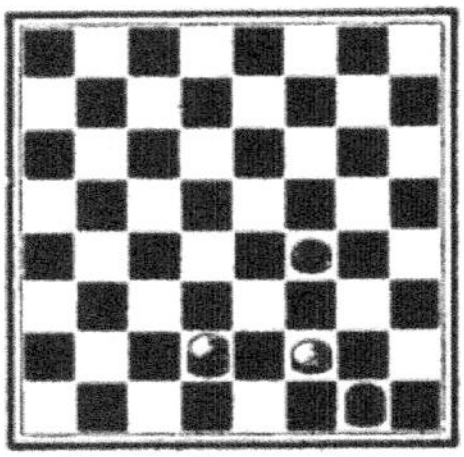

White to Play and Win

Position No. 2
By Samuel Gonotsky

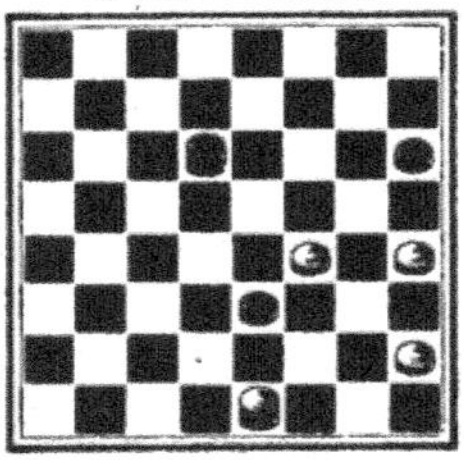

White to Play and Win

Position No. 3
By Tommie Wiswell

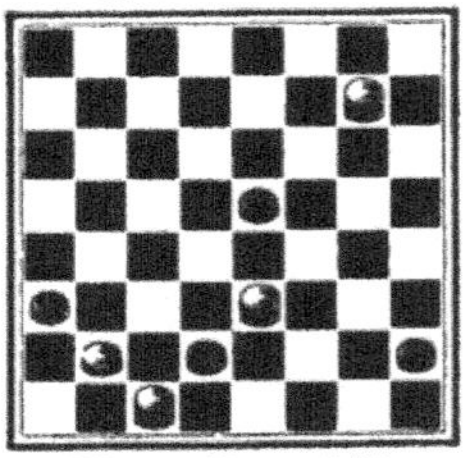

White to Play and Win

In our first lesson in end-game theory we deal with what is commonly known as the Double Corner Block. White corners a black king and single man in his double corner with a lone king as shown in Position No. 1. It is a very pleasing as well as instructive theme and many beautiful problems have been built around it. Position No. 2 by the late Samuel Gonotsky, a former American Champion, is a perfect illustration and Position No. 3 is another nice setting. Try to solve all three problems without looking at the solutions, which are given below.

Solutions

Position No. 1

27-24, 19-28, 26-23. White wins.

Position No. 2

20-16, 10-7—A, 28-24, 23-27, 31-26, 27-32, 19-15, 12-28, 26-23. White wins.

A. 10-14, 16-11, 14-10, 28-24, 23-27, 31-26, 27-32, 26-23, 32-28, 23-18, 28-32, 18-15, 10-6, 11-8. White wins.

Position No. 3

8-11, 26-31, 11-18, 31-26, 23-27, 26-23—A, 18-22, 23-32, 30-26, 21-30, 26-23. White wins.

A. If 26-22, 18-23, 22-29, 27-32 White wins.

Lesson Number 2

"NIPPED AT THE WIRE"

Position No. 1
(The Basic Idea)

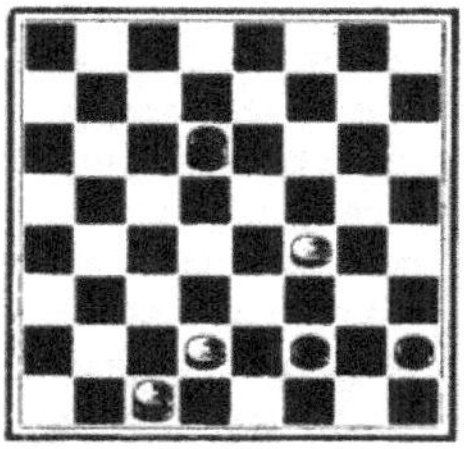

White to Play and Win

Position No. 2
By Chris Nelson

White to Play and Win

Position No. 3
By Peter Bennett

White to Play and Win

While the idea illustrated in our second lesson may not be quite as spectacular as the double corner block it is just as important and well worth knowing. We give two very pretty examples of this theme by two famous problemists. The ending in Position No. 2 was the subject of some analysis by a group of well known New York players at the Brooklyn Checker Club. Just as they were about to leave it off as a draw Mr. Nelson spied the cute win. The final position is by a composer who was famous in another era. He published many fine endings with only the initials P B signed to them.

Solutions

Position No. 1

19-15, 10-19, 26-23, 19-26, 30-32. White wins.

Position No. 2

9-14, 18-23, 14-18, 23-26 (If 27-32, 18-27, 32-23 White wins by First Position), 25-30, 26-31, 11-16, 12-19, 18-23, 19-26, 30-32. White wins.

Position No. 3

4-8, 1-6, 8-11, 6-10, 31-26, 23-27, 11-15, 10-19, 26-23, 19-26, 30-32. White wins.

Lesson Number 3

"THE ROYAL SACRIFICE"

Position No. 1
(The Basic Idea)

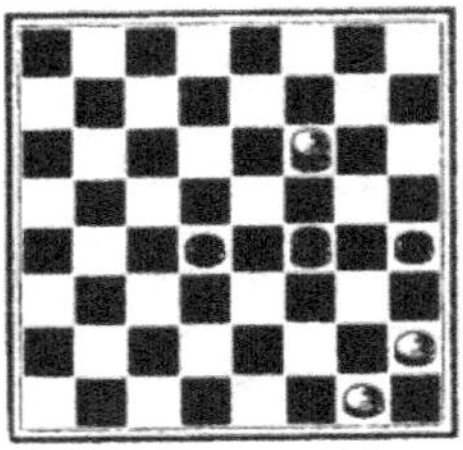

White to Play and Win

Position No. 2
By Chris Nelson

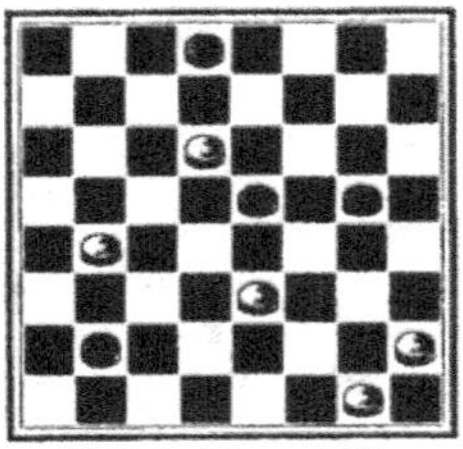

White to Play and Win

Position No. 3
By Tommie Wiswell

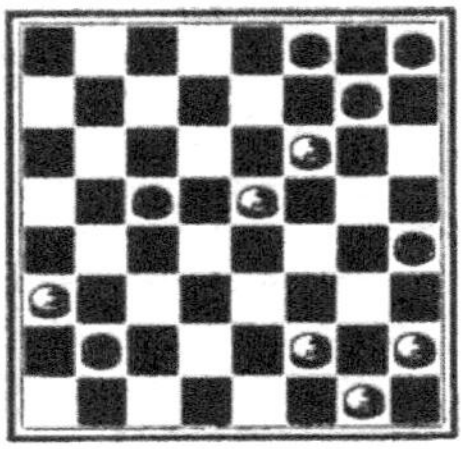

White to Play and Draw

The win in Position No. 1 is a real fooler and many experts have missed it in actual play. The great Newell W. Banks overlooked the idea in a recent exhibition game. We present another of Chris Nelson's gems in Position No. 2. It is a splendid example of this theme. Position No. 3 appeared not long ago as a cover problem for The American Checkerist. It is a difficult problem but since you already know the idea that is involved you should be able to solve it after a bit of study.

Solutions

Position No. 1
11-15, 19-10, 28-24. White wins.

Position No. 2
17-13, 25-30, 10-6, 2-9, 13-6, 30-26, 6-2, 26-19, 2-7, 16-20, 7-11, 15-18, 11-15, etc. White wins.

Position No. 3
27-23, 25-30, 23-19, 30-26, 11-7, 3-10, 15-6, 26-23, 6-2 (If 19-16, 8-12 White wins and if 19-15, 23-18 White wins), 23-16, 2-6, 16-19, 6-10, 14-18, 10-15, 19-10, 28-24. Drawn.

Lesson Number 4

"CHANGING THE GUARD"

Position No. 1
(The Basic Idea)

White to Play and Win

Position No. 2
By C. M. Wilder

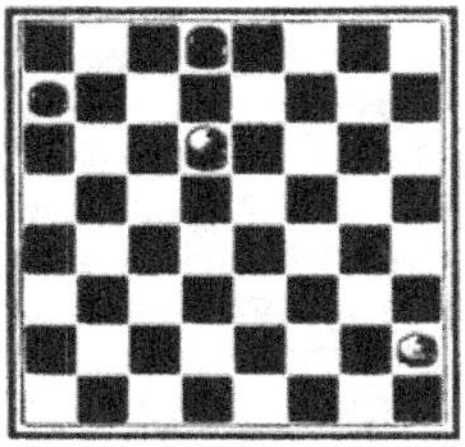

White to Play and Win

Position No. 3
By Chris Nelson

White to Play and Win

The maneuver shown in this lesson is very aptly called "Changing the guard" and you will realize why after you have solved Positions No. 1 and 2. For the third time we present one of Chris Nelson's practical positions. This time it is an actual ending that came up between two New York experts. In the game the player handling the white pieces allowed a draw and Chris, who happened to be an interested spectator, pointed out the correct route to the win.

Solutions

Position No. 1
10-14, 17-22, 15-10. White wins.

Position No. 2
28-24, 5-9, 24-19, 9-13, 19-15, 13-17, 10-14, 17-22, 15-10. White wins.

Position No. 3
2-6 (If 12-16, 19-24, 28-19, 18-15 Drawn), 26-30, 12-16, 30-25 (forced), 16-14, 22-26, 31-22, 25-2 and White wins as shown in Position No. 2.

Lesson Number 5

"BETWEEN THE DEVIL AND THE DEEP"

Position No. 1
(The Basic Idea)

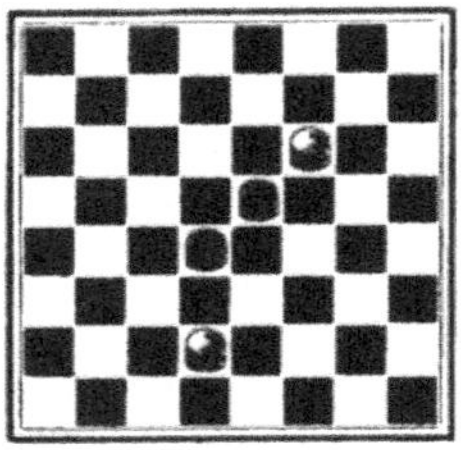

White to Play and Win

Position No. 2
(Selected)

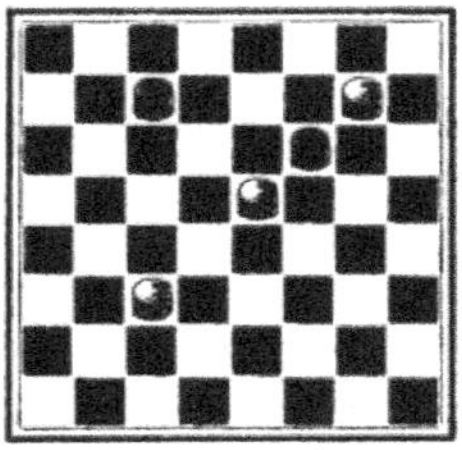

White to Play and Win

Position No. 3
By Fred Allen

White to Play and Win

In Position No. 1 Black, with an easy draw at hand, has just made a fatal error by playing 10-15. This is a very simple trap yet it is surprising how many players fall into it. It is a mistake that is usually committed by the novice who is over anxious to win. While the next two positions are not quite as simple, they are won on the same principle.

Solutions

Position No. 1

26-22 and either way Black jumps White wins.

Position No. 2

15-10, 6-15, 22-18, etc. White wins.

Position No. 3

27-23, 3-7, 4-8, 7-11, 15-10, 6-15, 23-18, 11-4, 18-11. White wins.

Lesson Number 6

"CAPTIVE COSSACKS"

Example No. 1
(The Basic Idea)

White to Play and Win

Example No. 2
By F. J. Hospidor

White to Play and Win

Example No. 3
By James Wyllie

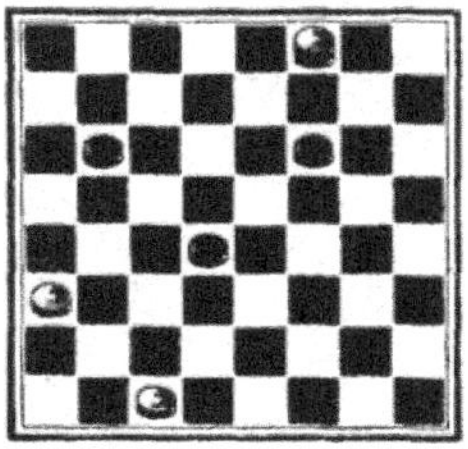

White to Play and Win

Many beautiful maneuvers may be executed on the checkerboard but few are more appealing or thrilling than the "Captive Cossacks" theme. This idea often arises in actual play. Example No. 2 is an ending that Mr. Hospidor won in a recent Washington, D. C. tournament. Example No. 3 is by the famous "Herd Laddie" who was Champion of the World for forty years.

Solutions

Position No. 1

26-22, 17-26, 27-31. White wins.

Position No. 2

31-26, 17-21, 26-22, 14-17, 23-27 (or 29-25), 17-26, 29-25, 30-21, 27-31. White wins.

Position No. 3

3-7, 11-16, 7-11, 16-20, 11-15, 18-23, 15-18, 23-27, 21-17, 9-13, 18-23, 13-22, 23-32, 20-24, 32-28, 24-27, 30-26, 22-31, 28-32. White wins.

Lesson Number 7

"HERDING TO THE SIDE"

Position No. 1
(The Basic Idea)

White to Play and Draw.

Position No. 2
By Robert Martins

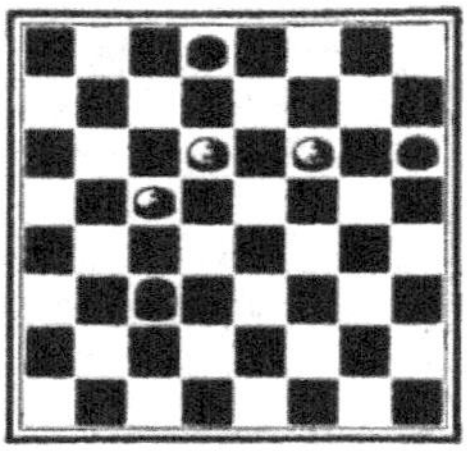

White to Play and Draw

Position No. 3
By Tommie Wiswell

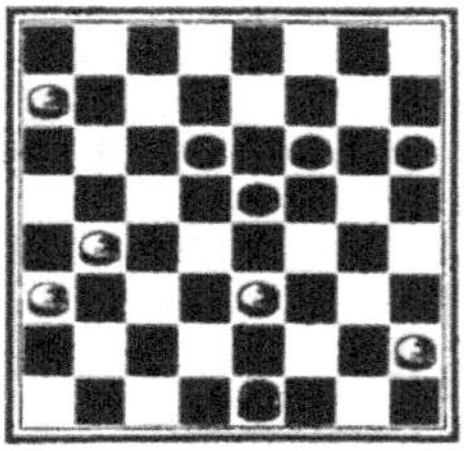

White to Play and Draw

The student will discover from time to time that there are various ways that one king can draw against two opposing men. In this lesson we deal with a man down draw that is of frequent occurrence in actual play. You will be able to save many games that looks hopeless once you have mastered this idea.

Solutions

Position No. 1

14-10, 11-16, 10-15, 16-20, 15-19. Drawn.

Position No. 2

14-9, 22-18, 9-5, 18-15, 11-7, 2-11, 5-1, 15-6, 1-10, etc. Drawn.

Position No. 3

5-1, 31-27, 23-19, 15-24, 28-19, 27-24, 17-14, 10-17, 21-14, 24-15, 14-10, 15-6, 1-10. Drawn.

Lesson Number 8

"PERPETUAL CHECK"

Position No. 1
(The Basic Idea)

White to Play and Draw

Position No. 2
By A. Ross

White to Play and Draw

Position No. 3
By E. Svenning

White to Play and Draw

In the previous lesson the reader saw how one King could draw against two single men. There are times when one King can also draw against two enemy Monarchs. As the student will observe from the above positions the idea in these situations is to confine the two opposing Kings in one of the single corners and force a see-saw draw or perpetual check. The tactics which bring about the draw in position number three are pleasing and instructive.

Solutions

Position No. 1

15-11. Drawn: as the two Kings are hemmed in and Black can only move 12-8, 8-3, 3-8, etc. Try it.

Position No. 2

15-10, 19-12, 6-2, 14-7, 2-11. Drawn.

Position No. 3

26-22, 18-25, 21-17, 1-5, 9-6, 2-9, 17-13, 9-14, 13-9, 14-7, 8-3, 5-14, 3-17. Drawn.

Lesson Number 9

"THE ACE IN THE HOLE"

Position No. 1
(The Basic Idea)

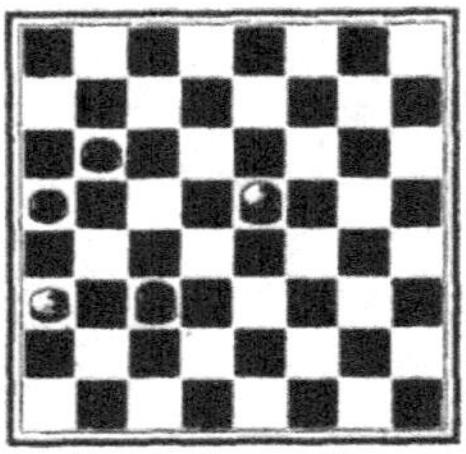

White to Play and Draw

Position No. 2
By E. A. Jones

White to Play and Draw

Position No. 3
By Ben Boland

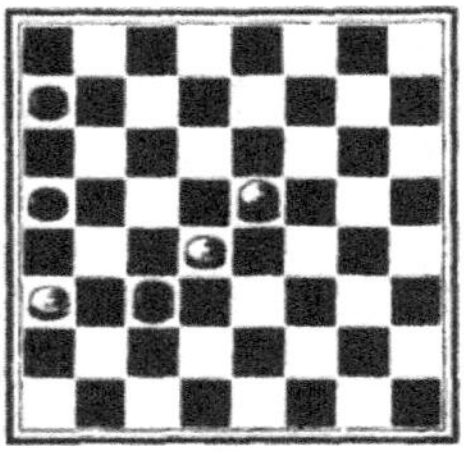

White to Play and Win

Sometimes one little move can change what looks like a hopeless loss into a well earned draw. A move of this type is illustrated in Positions Nos. 1 and 2. If you will take the Whites in the first diagram and make the correct move you will leave Blacks with only one move to draw. In Problem No. 3 a neat win is brought off by utilizing this idea. The author of this position is a famous authority on end-game play.

Solutions

Position No. 1

21-17. Drawn. As a matter of fact Black must now play 9-14 in order to draw as 22-25 and 22-26 both lose by 17-14.

Position No. 2

17-13, 30-25, 22-17, 25-21, 13-9 (If 17-14, 1-6 Black wins), 21-14, 3-7. Drawn.

Position No. 3

18-14, 22-25, 14-10, 25-22, 10-6, 5-9, 21-17. White wins.

Lesson Number 10

"THE DOUBLE STEAL"

Position No. 1
(The Basic Idea)

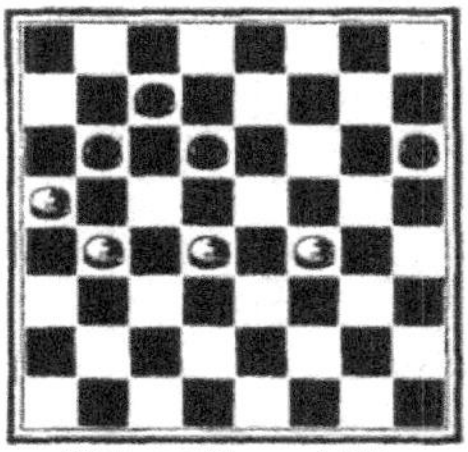

White to Play and Win

Position No. 2
By Charles Hefter

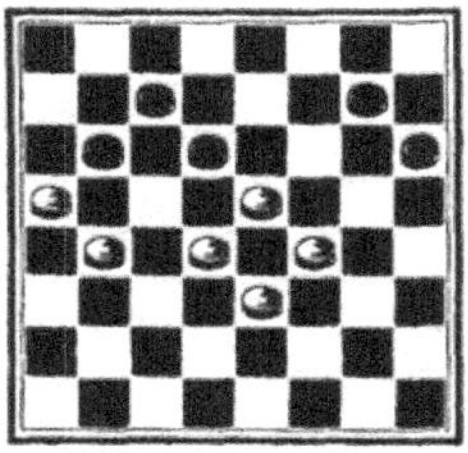

White to Play and Draw

Position No. 3
By Tommie Wiswell

White to Play and Win

The beginner will do well to learn the art of sacrificing early in his checker career. That is the moral of this lesson. Often the giving up of one, two and sometimes even three men will enable you to draw or win a game, as the case may be. Although White gives up from one to three pieces in each of the above positions, in all three cases Black cannot save the two men on squares 6 and 9. Position No. 2 was left as a Black win in an old checker magazine but Mr. Hefter pointed out the neat draw.

Solutions

Position No. 1

19-15, 10-19, 17-14, 19-23, 14-5 and White wins as the man on 6 is doomed.

Position No. 2

15-11, 8-22, 23-18, 22-26, 19-15, 10-19, 17-14, 26-31, 14-5, 6-10, 5-1, 31-26, 1-6. Drawn.

Position No. 3

11-7, 15-22, 30-25, 2-11, 25-18, 4-8, 29-25, 8-12, 25-21, 12-16, 21-17 (18-15 only draws), 16-19, 20-16, 11-20, 16-19. White wins.

Lesson Number 11

"THE SINGLE CORNER BLOCK"

Position No. 1
(The Basic Idea)

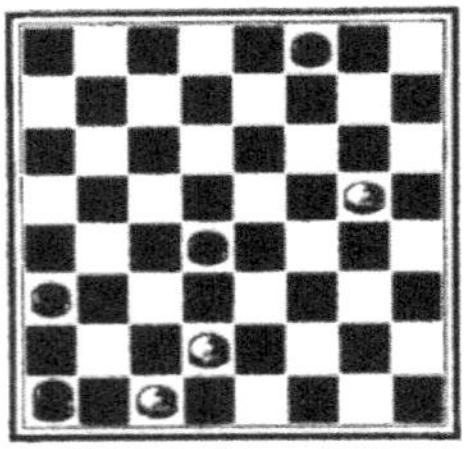

White to Play and Win

Position No. 2
(Selected)

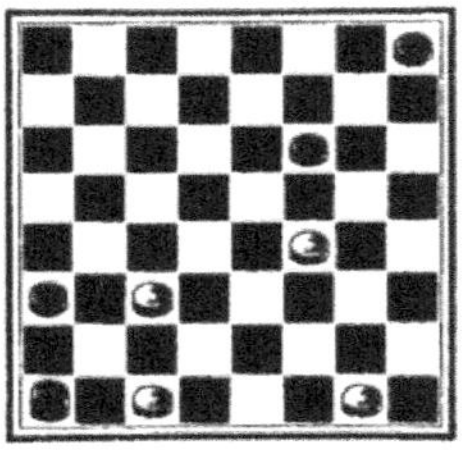

White to Play and Win

Position No. 3
By Julius D'Orio

White to Play and Win

In our first lesson we studied the Double Corner Block and now we take up what is known as the Single Corner Block. This is another very spectacular method of winning a game and never fails to delight the novice. You will undoubtedly solve Positions Nos. 1 and 2 without much difficulty but beware of Mr. D'Orio's problem. This is a real gem by the veteran Pacific Coast expert and author.

Solutions

Position No. 1

26-22, 18-25, 16-11. White wins.

Position No. 2

19-15, 11-25, 32-27, 4-8, 27-23, 8-11, 23-19. White wins.

Position No. 3

26-22, 18-25, 2-7, 12-16, 7-11, 16-19, 32-27, 28-32 (19-23 also loses), 11-16, 32-23, 30-26. White wins.

KING ENDINGS

Many beginners have considerable trouble winning when they have two kings to their opponent's one king. This is a very simple matter and is done as follows (See Diagram A):

Two Kings vs. One King
Diagram A

White to Play and Win

Three Kings vs. Two Kings
Diagram B

Either to Play, White Wins

In Diagram A the idea is to force the lone Black king out of the double corner like this: 14-9, 1-5, 10-14, 5-1, 9-5, 1-6, 5-1, 6-2, 14-18, 2-7, 18-15, 7-2, 15-11. White wins.

While winning three kings against two is a little tougher job it is not very hard once you learn how to do it. (See Diagram B.) It is especially easy if the two kings are in the same double corner as in Diagram B. First let us suppose it is White's move. In that case the win would be as follows: 16-19, 27-31 (If 27-24, 20-27, 32-16, 28-24 White wins on the move), 20-24, 32-27, 28-32, 27-20, 19-24, 20-27, 32-23. White wins. Should Black move first from Diagram B the win would go like this: 27-31, 20-24, 32-27, (If 31-26, 16-19 White wins), 16-19, 27-20, 28-32. White wins.

Three Kings vs. Two Kings
Diagram C

White to Play and Win

Four Kings vs. Three Kings
Diagram D

White to Play and Win

Diagram C is another version of three kings against two. Many players are under the impression that the three kings cannot win against the two kings when the latter occupy both double corners as in this case. As a matter of fact White can force a win easily. Here are the key moves to the White win: 18-15, 24-28, 23-27—A, 6-1, 14-10, 28-32, 27-24, 1-5 (If 32-28, 24-19, 28-32, 10-6 White wins), 10-6, 5-1, 24-19. White wins.

A. Note that with this move White threatens to make a trade should Black play 28-32. With every move White now makes *an exchange is threatened*, which exchange in the end is neatly forced. Remember that one king moves on squares 15 and 18. Another king moves (when necessary) on squares 6, 9, 10, and 14, the third king controls and moves (when necessary) on squares 19, 23, 24, and 27.

Many strong players encounter trouble in winning with four kings against three as depicted in Diagram D. This is how it is done: 20-24, 32-28, 23-19, 28-32, 24-28, 31-27, 19-16, 27-31, 16-20, 31-27 (If 32-27, 28-32, 27-23, 20-24. White wins), 22-26, 30-23, 28-24, 27-31, 24-27, 31-24, 20-18. White wins.

PROBLEM SECTION

EDITED BY

TOMMIE WISWELL

WITH CONTRIBUTIONS BY

CHARLES HEFTER
CHRIS NELSON
BEN BOLAND
FAUSTO DALUMI
THE LATE A. J. HEFFNER
THE LATE SAMUEL GONOTSKY
L. J. VAIR
JESSE B. HANSON
PAUL R. SEMPLE
LOUIS C. GINSBERG
NORMAN CLARK
WILLIAM J. WOOD
JACK GORDON
JAMES MOIR
E. J. REES
THE PROBLEM EDITOR
AND
VARIOUS AUTHORS OF NOTE

THE STUDY OF PROBLEMS

Any textbook on checkers would be sadly incomplete without a department devoted to problems. No player ever reached the expert or master class without making a deep study of end-games and problems of all kinds.

Problem solving is to checker players what training and punching the bag is to the prize fighter—preliminary practice to actual combat. Every boxer knows that his chances of success are mighty slim if he enters the ring out of shape and without proper training. The checker player who hopes to play even a fair game must also train and practice many hours before he is mentally fit for the fray.

The student who conscientiously studies the positions given in the following pages and successfully works out the solutions will be more than repaid for his efforts. Besides passing away many enjoyable hours, his cross-board ability and powers of visualizations will, we are confident, improve to a marked degree.

The reader will find that all types of problems have been included to satisfy his taste, strokes, end-games, blocks, etc. Some of them will be found easy. Others will prove to be harder, while a few will probably stump you, but all will, we hope, prove beneficial and pleasing. If stymied, you can always look at the answers in the back of the book—but we hope you don't.

Note: All positions in the Problem Section are set with the side to move at the bottom of the board.

TOMMIE WISWELL.

AN ALL-AMERICAN PROBLEMIST TEAM

"Who are America's greatest living problemists?" (Asks the Checker Editor of the Roseville Citizen.) On what basis can we select such a team? We'd like to be able to answer such a question fairly for we believe it would please a devotee of problem composing to learn how much his compositions are appreciated—while he is living.

Some great players have composed problems which are masterpieces—probably only a few—yet they do not consider themselves problemists. In classifying problemists we must consider among other things:

1. Greatest demonstrated knowledge of end-game themes.

2. Greatest analytical ability.

3. The precision, exactitude and beauty of the problemist's works.

4. Record for fewest corrections.

5. Naturalness of settings.

6. Prolific, consistent publication of good problems.

Taking into consideration the above and in a spirit of appreciation of all problemists for their prodigious efforts at gem making and for their many excellent contributions to the literature of the game we present our choice for the All-American Problemist Team. (Arranged Alphabetically.)

1. Bert Berry, Lincoln, Nebraska
2. Ben Boland, Brooklyn, New York
3. Fausto Dalumi, New York City, N. Y.
4. Jack Gordon, Brooklyn, New York
5. Charles Hefter, Kankakee, Ill.
6. Frank A. Miller, Seattle, Washington
7. Chris Nelson, Brooklyn, New York
8. Paul R. Semple, Martins Ferry, Ohio
9. L. J. Vair, Denver, Colo.
10. Tommie Wiswell, New York City, N. Y.

Other worthwhile candidates for the team are: Maurice Shapiro, L. S. Hart, Bert E. Sanderson, Tom LaRacy, C. A. Woodard, Miles R. Smith, Norman H. Clark, T. Quinlan, John McGrath, George L. King, William Fleming, W. J. Wood, Milton Loew, Milton Johnson and several others.

Problem No. 1
(PAL)

White to Play and Draw

By TOMMIE WISWELL

This Prize Problem was a great favorite of the young members of the P. A. L. (Police Athletic League) in New York City where Mr. Grover was an Instructor. He later included it in a booklet he wrote for their Department of Recreation. We've nicknamed it "PAL" in their honor.

Problem No. 2

White to Play and Draw

By TOMMIE WISWELL

White is a man down in this problem and has to make quite a few star moves to get the draw. The theme is treated in Lesson No. 9 of the end-game section.

Problem No. 3

White to Play and Win

By TOMMIE WISWELL

Although the White forces are three men ahead, they just barely win in this position. A rather unusual but very instructive setting.

Problem No. 4
(Black Magic)

Black to Play and Win

By TOMMIE WISWELL

This position first appeared as a cover problem for The American Checkerist where it was given the picturesque title "Black Magic" by the Editor. Despite this imposing name, it is more amusing than difficult.

Problem No. 5

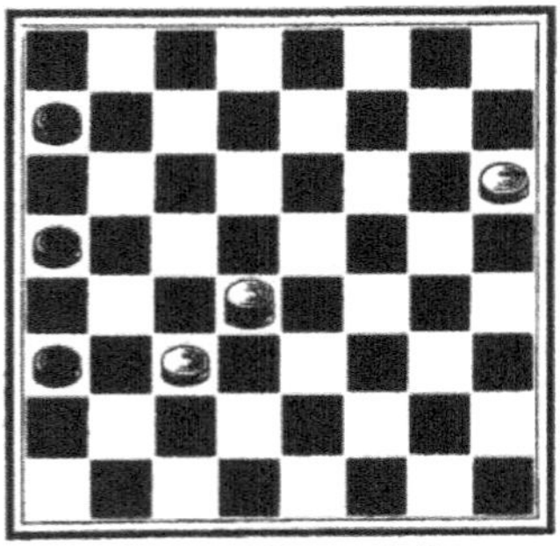

White to Play and Win

By TOMMIE WISWELL

This is a simple little fellow although the win was missed in actual play. Can you do it? Remember, don't touch the pieces.

Problem No. 6

White to Play and Win

By TOMMIE WISWELL

The theme of this problem was also treated on in the end-game section, but we're not going to say where—we'll leave that for you to find out.

Problem No. 7

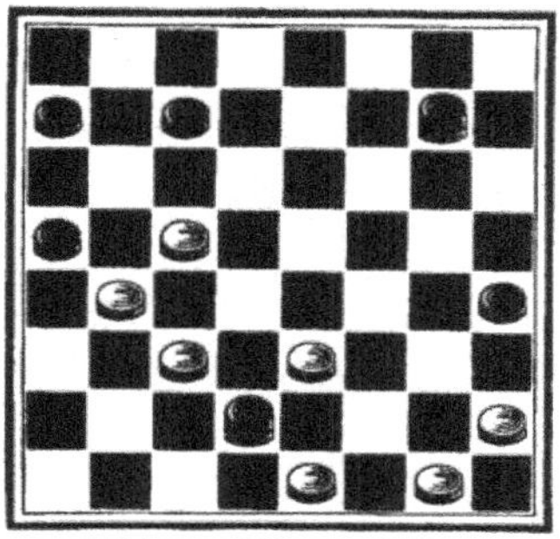

White to Play and Win

By TOMMIE WISWELL

You'll get a real "kick" out of this one. The solution is short and snappy and the "key" move is quite a shock—to Black.

Problem No. 8

White to Play and Win

By TOMMIE WISWELL

Here is another cover problem from The American Checkerist. White goes a man down again to force a very pretty win. Now we've given you a hint regarding the solution.

Problem No. 9

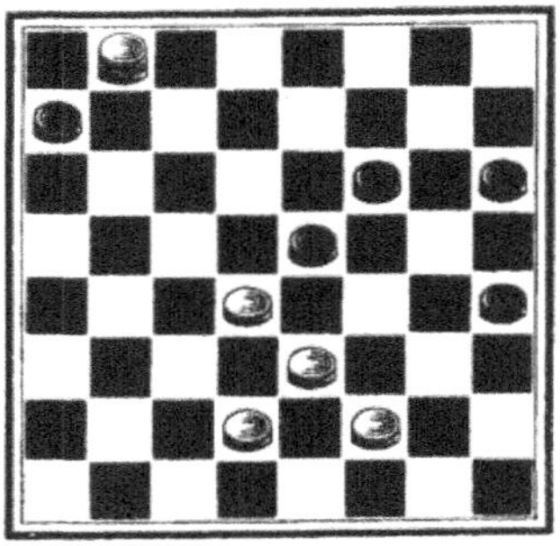

White to Play and Draw

By TOMMIE WISWELL

This is one of the earliest problems published by the writer and is another position from an actual game. You will find the solution both pleasing and practical.

Problem No. 10

White to Play and Win

By TOMMIE WISWELL

While this prize problem has a very natural appearance, it is actually a composition. Here is another occasion where Black gets a big shock.

Problem No. 11
(Five Star Finale)

White to Play and Win

By TOMMIE WISWELL

We feel that it is only fair to warn you regarding Problems No. 11 and 12. Both are "tough nuts to crack," but a little perseverance will do it. The solution to No. 11 calls for five star moves, hence its title.

Problem No. 12

White to Play and Draw

By TOMMIE WISWELL

As can be seen from the diagram, this is a stroke problem and purely a composition. Harry Lieberman, the noted Internationalist, called this one of the neatest stroke problems in checkers.

TO CHARLES HEFTER

"Dean of American Problemists"

Sitting at the checker board,
  Bewildered and perplexed,
Struggling with a problem there
  Which has our soul so vexed;

It seems so simple, yet, forsooth,
  We've tried in every way
To solve this most elusive cuss
  With every kind of play.

We look up at the author's name,
  One versed in checker lore,
Then hand again across the board
  To try once more.

Let's see, white's king's on seven,
  Now get this problem straight;
A single piece on twenty-five,
  And one on twenty-eight.

Black has a king on fourteen,
  Intent on playing tricks;
Supporting him, he pieces has
  On nineteen and twenty-six.

The terms are black to play and win
  A choice bit rich and rare,
And in Gould's Book of Problems
  We find the answer there.

Though many years have passed and gone
  Since on the Checker World
This problemist of genius first
  His gifted gems unfurled.

And since that time and through the years,
  In many a gem serene,
His gifted touch across the board,
  To our delight, is seen.

And as to you, Charles Hefter,
  We rise, A Checker Clan,
And toast to you, with hearts sincere,
  "Here's to our Grand Old Man."

TOM QUINLAN.

Problem No. 13

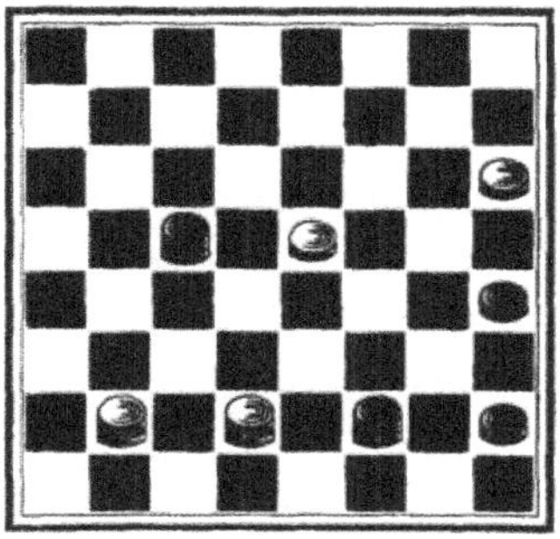

Black to Play and Win

By CHARLES HEFTER

Like practically all of Mr. Hefter's positions this one is a correction and first appeared in the Mt. Sterling (Kentucky) Advocate. Newell W. Banks rates the gentleman from Kankakee as "Public Critic No. 1." For over fifty years he has been active as player, analyst and critic.

Problem No. 14

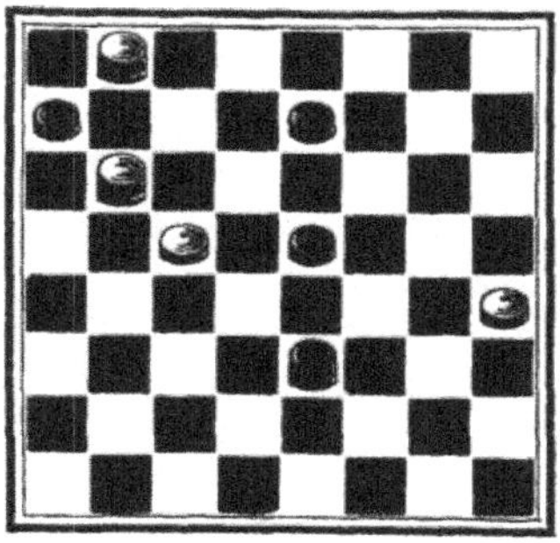

White to Play and Win

BY CHARLES HEFTER

Mr. Hefter claims that he never composed a problem in his life, that all his positions either came up in actual games or in analysis. We haven't the slightest doubt regarding the truth of this statement and can only conclude Mr. Hefter is a genius.

Problem No. 15

White to Play and Draw

By CHARLES HEFTER

We consider this one of Mr. Hefter's best problems—and that's saying a lot. The author demonstrates a very pretty draw that is quite practical.

Problem No. 16

Black to Play and Draw

By CHARLES HEFTER

The author demonstrates another useful draw in No. 16. Black must make a number of star moves to avoid defeat.

Problem No. 17

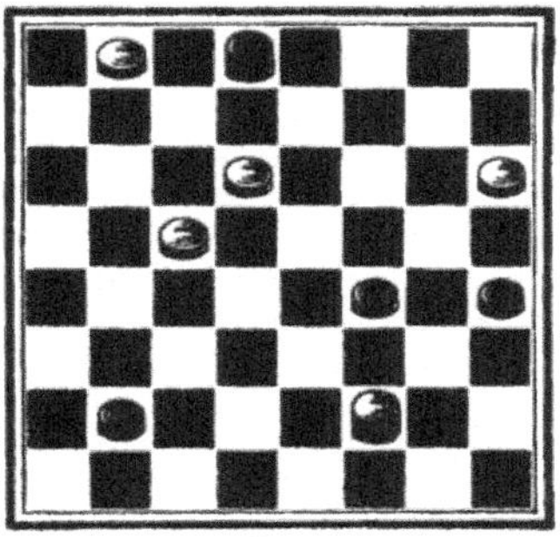

Black to Play and Draw

By CHARLES HEFTER

No. 17 has the typical Hefter touch. Any position by this author is a lesson in itself as he always shows a nice point. Of course, like all the author's positions, this one is from actual play.

Problem No. 18

Black to Play and Draw

By CHARLES HEFTER

Another nice correction is shown in No. 18. This time of a setting by W. J. Wood, Problem King of the National Checker Association. Mr. Hefter is no respecter of persons or titles.

Problem No. 19

White to Play and Draw

By CHARLES HEFTER

White does some nice forcing in this one and clinches the draw right down at the finish. Better late than never, says Mr. Hefter.

Problem No. 20

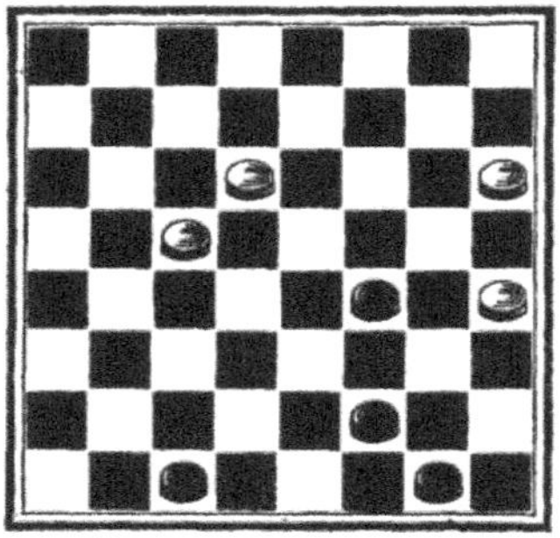

Black to Play and Win

By CHARLES HEFTER

Problem No. 20 is a Bradford-Pawlowski ending from the 1935 Illinois State Tourney which ended in a draw. The author pointed out the neat win shortly afterward.

Problem No. 21

White to Play and Win

By CHRIS NELSON

During the past few years, many fine problems have appeared in various checker columns under the nom-de-plume "The Deckhand." This modest composer is none other than the famous Chris Nelson of Brooklyn, whom many players contend is America's No. 1 problemist. Nelson, who is in a class by himself as an analyst and composer, has a keen sense of humor and many of his positions will make you smile.

By CHRIS NELSON

This problem has a very cute "joker" (fake solution) that has fooled many strong players. While the correct solution is really very simple, we doubt that you will get it the first time.

Problem No. 22

White to Play and Win

Problem No. 23

White to Play and Win

By CHRIS NELSON

Problem No. 23 is an ending from the single corner. Nelson's play to win as given in the solution is the only line of play with which White can score.

Problem No. 24

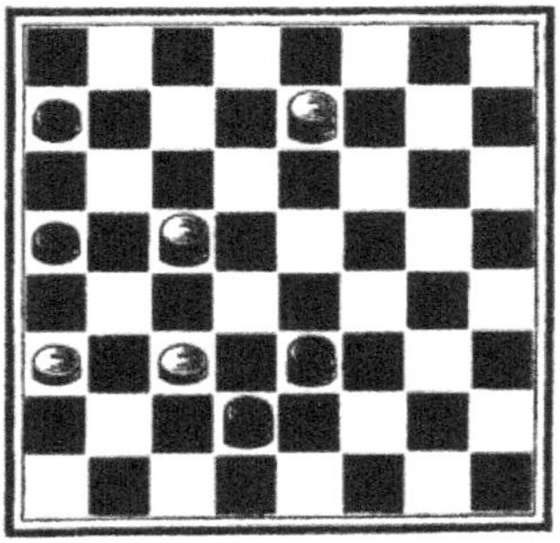

White to Play and Draw

By CHRIS NELSON

Although it is not generally known, "The Deckhand" is a strong crossboard player and in the days of the Brooklyn Checker Club engaged many of America's best players, always holding his own. Number 24 is the finish of a club game the author played with A. J. Mantell.

Problem No. 25

White to Play and Win

By CHRIS NELSON

Problem No. 25 is another ending the author had in a match game. This time with the noted Internationalist, John T. Bradford. Nelson piloted the White pieces to victory as per the solution.

Problem No. 26

White to Play and Win

By CHRIS NELSON

Problem No. 26 is purely a composition, and a very nice one you'll agree when you've solved it.

Problem No. 27

White to Play and Win

By CHRIS NELSON

Problem No. 27 is one of those apparently simple positions where it seems most anything will win. As a matter of fact, White is compelled to make a number of star moves that nine players out of ten would miss in an actual game.

Problem No. 28

White to Play and Win

By CHRIS NELSON

This interesting position came up between Bill Ferguson, a New York expert, and Willie Ryan at the Brooklyn Checker Club a few years back. Gonotsky and Ginsberg thought it a draw but Nelson shows a pretty win.

Problem No. 29

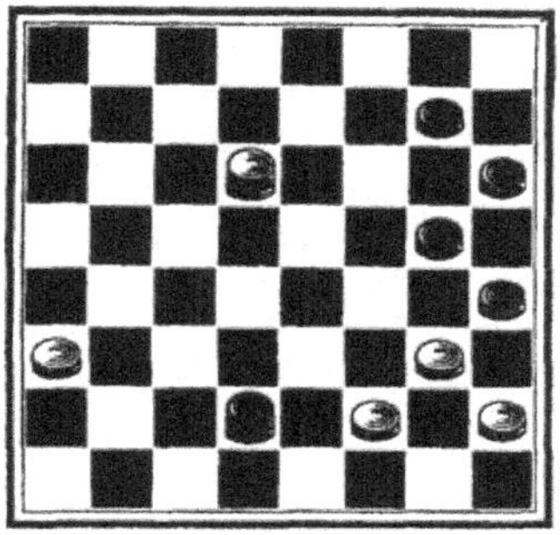

White to Play and Draw

By BEN BOLAND

The author of Problems 29–36 is considered America's foremost authority on Problem Themes. He is a native of Brooklyn and the author of several textbooks dealing with this department of the game. His "Familiar Themes in the Scientific Game of Checkers" is one of the recent outstanding contributions to the literature of the game.

By BEN BOLAND

There are some nice points to Problem 30. White can go wrong very easily, so watch your step.

Problem No. 30

White to Play and Draw

Problem No. 31

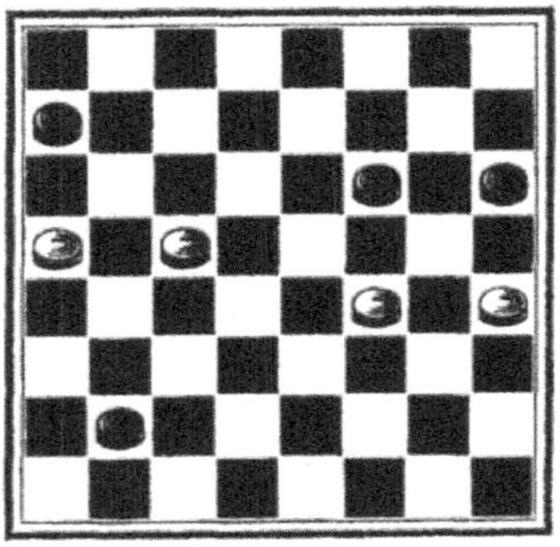

White to Play and Draw

By BEN BOLAND

Here is another fine study by the famous Brooklyn author. It is not an easy one, but you will be well repaid for your efforts should you solve it—without looking at the solution.

Problem No. 32

White to Play and Draw

By BEN BOLAND

All of this author's problems seem to have the same terms, either Black or White to draw. Mr. Boland could well be called "The Drawing Master."

Problem No. 33

White to Play and Draw

By BEN BOLAND

Mr. Boland shows us his lighter side in this little study. The idea is neat and instructive. You will solve it if you are not hasty.

Problem No. 34

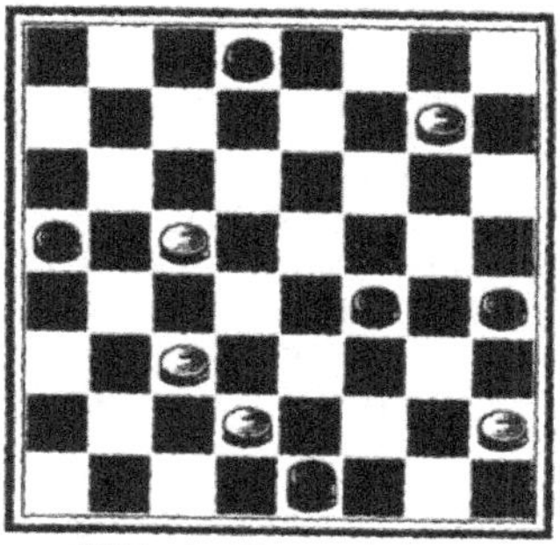

White to Play and Draw

By BEN BOLAND

White has to do some clever maneuvering to get the draw in No. 34. This type of positions is Mr. Boland's specialty.

Problem No. 35

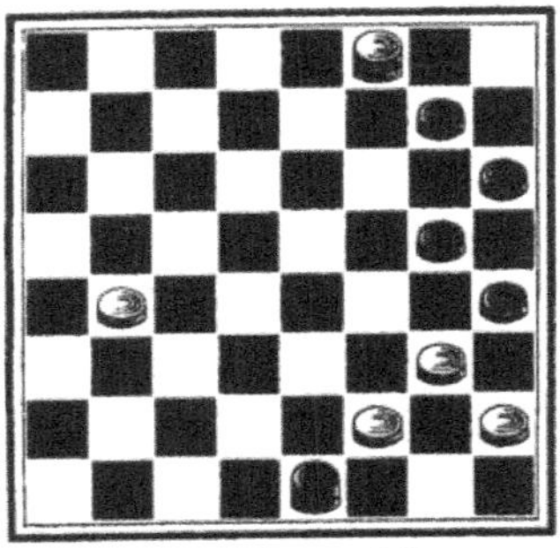

White to Play and Draw

By BEN BOLAND

It will be noted that this setting is akin to No. 29 by the same author. It is one of Mr. Boland's prize problems.

Problem No. 36

Black to Play, White Draws

By BEN BOLAND

This position corrects a note to Problem No. 1017 in Gould's problem book. A. J. Mantell, the noted New York player and analyst considers this one of the finest bridge positions in checkers.

By FAUSTO DALUMI

Problem No. 37

White to Play and Draw

Fausto Dalumi was born in Milan, Italy, but is now a citizen of the United States. "He is recognized as a past master in the art of problem composing and his works are equally noteworthy for their practicability, difficulty and elegance of construction. . . ." Thus does the Editor of The Draughts Review describe Mr. Dalumi's problems and it is a description with which we are in full agreement. Many of the notes regarding the ten problems that follow are by the author. Number 37 first appeared in The Roseville Citizen, November 7, 1929.

Problem No. 38

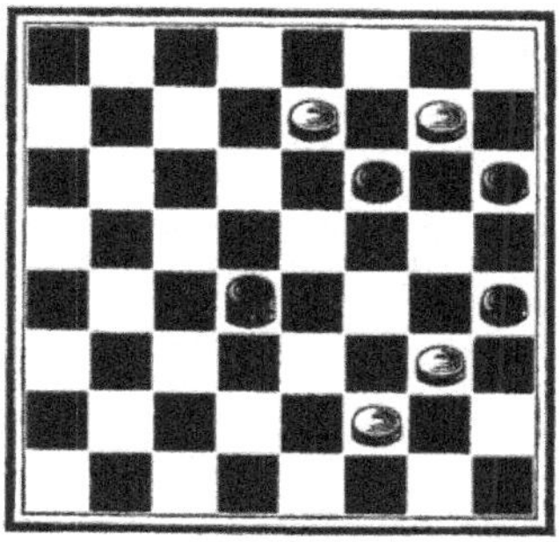

White to Play and Draw

By FAUSTO DALUMI

Problem No. 38 is one of the author's many prize problems. Only the sacrifice will draw.

Problem No. 39

White to Play and Win

By FAUSTO DALUMI

All the moves must be properly timed in Problem No. 39. As Mr. Dalumi says in the solution "every White move is 'starred.'" This feature is characteristic of many of this author's problems.

Problem No. 40

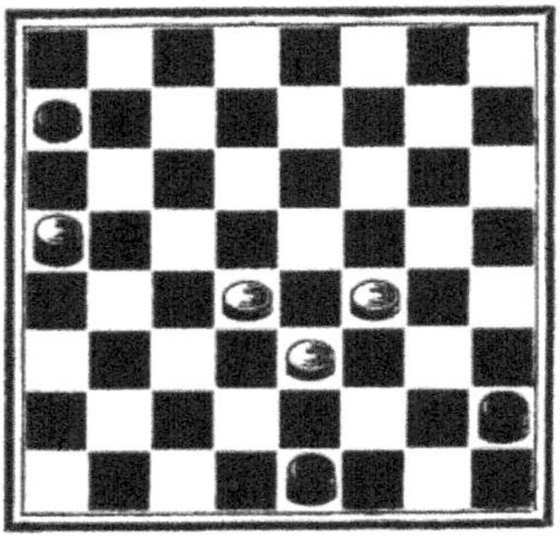

White to Play and Win

By FAUSTO DALUMI

Position No. 40 is another of the author's prize problems. This time from the columns of the Boston Evening Globe, May 11, 1929.

Problem No. 41

White to Play and Draw

By FAUSTO DALUMI

Many fine players claimed that Problem No. 41 was a Black win when it first appeared; but, the author proves otherwise in his solution.

Problem No. 42

White to Play and Draw

By FAUSTO DALUMI

Problem No. 42 is another position that calls for correct timing. All of Mr. Dalumi's problems are instructive and show points that the student should note closely. They are of far more value to the player who wishes to make a scientific study of the game than spectacular and artificial strokes.

Problem No. 43

White to Play and Draw

By FAUSTO DALUMI

The author states that Problem No. 43 was first published in the "Portland Evening Express," November 1, 1919. Once again all of White's moves are "starred."

Problem No. 44

White to Play and Draw

By FAUSTO DALUMI

Position No. 44 makes a very fine study and can honestly be described as a gem. It is the type of problem that has made the author famous throughout the checker world.

Problem No. 45

White to Play and Draw

By FAUSTO DALUMI

Problem No. 45 is a position from an actual game. White played 10-14 and lost, but 10-7 draws neatly. We've told you the initial move, the rest is up to you.

Problem No. 46

White to Play and Win

By FAUSTO DALUMI

On very rare occasions Mr. Dalumi tries his hand at stroke problems. If all problems of this type were as good as No. 46 the stroke problem would have a much better reputation than it has today. A real treat for those who like "fire works."

Problem No. 47

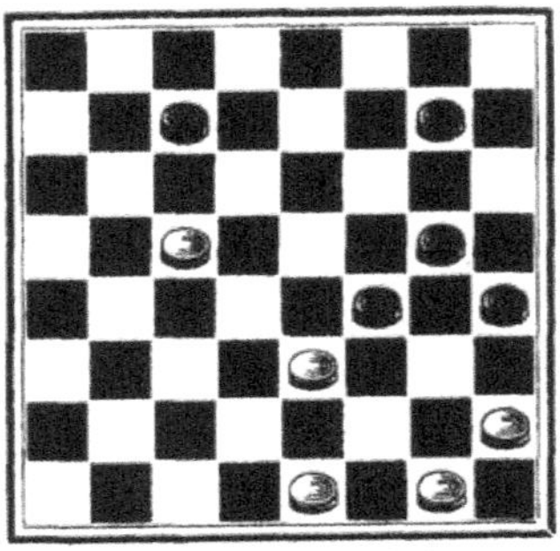

White to Play and Win

By A. J. HEFFNER

The late A. J. Heffner of Boston was one of the few great players who was also a great problemist. He was a former American Champion and a member of the All-American teams that played Great Britain (1905 and 1927). He served as team coach as well as a player on the 1927 team. Heffner was truly an all-around checkerist. He excelled as player, problemist, analyst, publisher and promoter.

By A. J. HEFFNER

Problem No. 48 is one of the great classics of the checker board. This little collection of Heffner's works would hardly be complete without it. If we were asked to select the best problem we had ever seen this one would be our choice.

Problem No. 48

White to Play and Win

Problem No. 49

White to Play and Draw

By A. J. HEFFNER

Number 49 is a nice study for those who appreciate delicate maneuvering. Heffner greatly enjoyed setting up this type of brain teaser for a group of players at the club.

Problem No. 50

White to Play and Win

By A. J. HEFFNER

White, a piece ahead in No. 50, makes the most of his numerical superiority and brings the game to a very pretty finish.

Problem No. 51

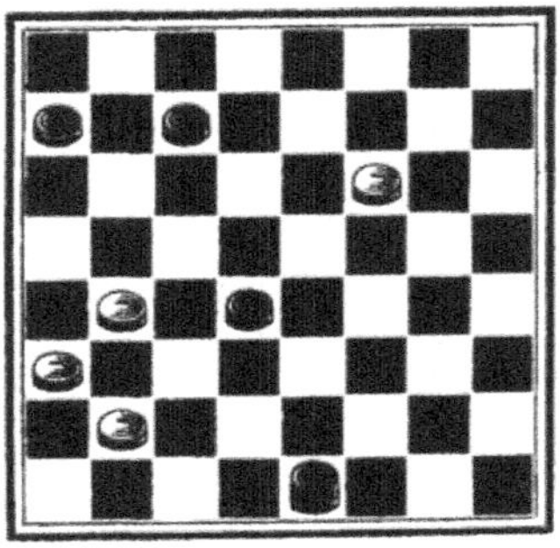

White to Play and Draw

By A. J. HEFFNER

This neat position first appeared in the columns of the Roseville (New Jersey) Citizen. Many of Heffner's gems first appeared in the checker department of this newspaper.

Problem No. 52

White to Play and Draw

By A. J. HEFFNER

This position is a fine correction of published play. The critics all thought it was a Black win but Mr. Heffner showed a clever escape for White.

Problem No. 53

White to Play and Draw

By SAMUEL GONOTSKY

While the late Samuel Gonotsky did not publish many problems in his brief and brilliant career, the few that he did contribute to various columns and magazines were ample proof of his wonderful ability. In our opinion the title of the World's greatest player belonged to either Richard Jordan or Gonotsky. He was a former American Champion and seemed headed for the World's Title when he died in 1929, still in his early twenties. His match with M. Lieber of Detroit (forty games, all drawn) is one of the greatest contests in checker history.

By SAMUEL GONOTSKY

Problem No. 54 is an ending from the Fife that the author had with Jesse B. Hanson. These two masters played many games with each other with the honors about even.

Problem No. 54

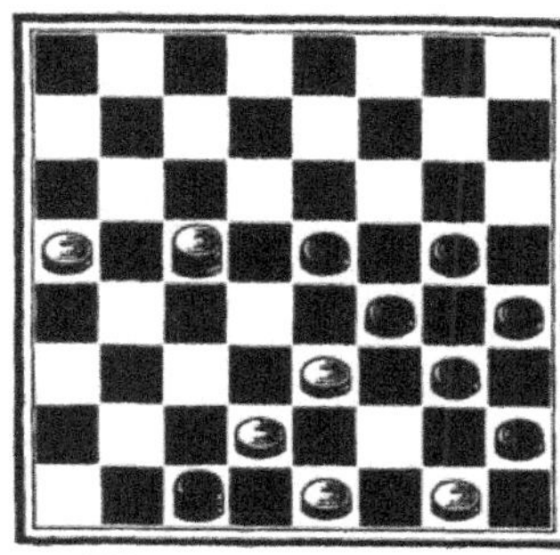

White to Play and Draw

Problem No. 55

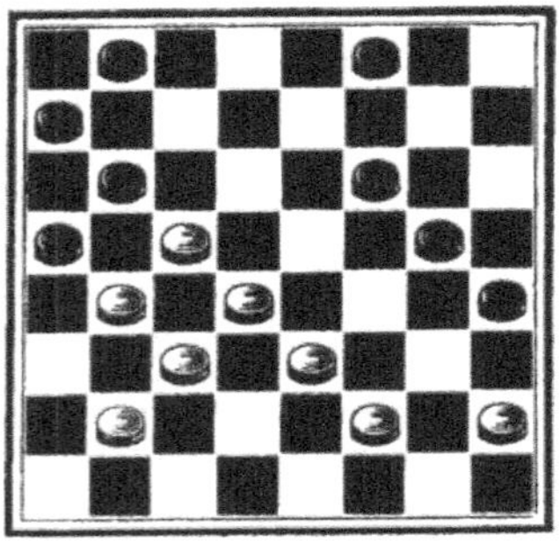

White to Play and Draw

By SAMUEL GONOTSKY

No. 55 is a difficult study, best suited for the advanced player. It is a very nice correction of published play and first appeared in the Draughts Review.

Problem No. 56

White to Play and Draw

By SAMUEL GONOTSKY

After a problem like No. 55 something lighter is in order and we have just the thing in No. 56. A very pretty draw, from actual play.

Problem No. 57

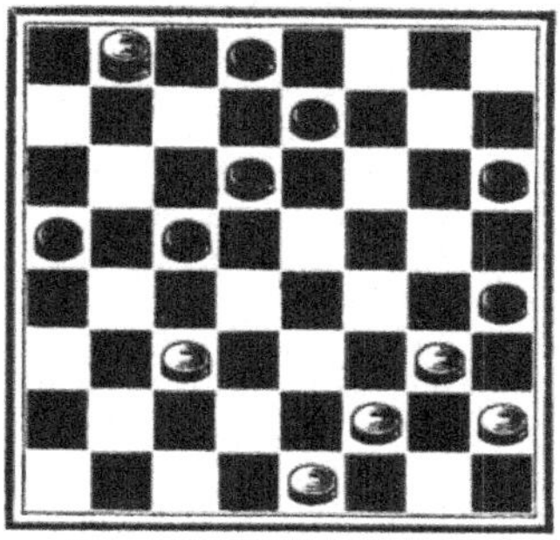

White to Play and Draw

By SAMUEL GONOTSKY

Another very fine ending from one of Gonotsky's games. It seemed that every game Sammie played was a brilliancy. This was no doubt due to the fact that his play was always deep and enterprising, never dry or dull.

Problem No. 58

White to Play and Draw

By SAMUEL GONOTSKY

Number 58 is a position that has been widely acclaimed. It is a delightful and instructive position that will appeal to the novice and expert alike.

Problem No. 59

White to Play and Win

By L. J. VAIR

"The Kolorado Kowboy" (L. J. Vair) of Denver has probably published more fine problems during the past quarter of a century than any other player in the world. Mr. Vair's offerings have a peculiar style of their own. They are light and airy and never fail to please the student. Problem No. 59 is a typical "Vair Vignette."

By L. J. VAIR

The author demonstrates a very unusual win in No. 60. It is this type of problem that is Mr. Vair's specialty.

Problem No. 60

White to Play and Win

Problem No. 61

White to Play and Win

By L. J. VAIR

Here is as pleasing a little problem as one could wish for. Though White is a man ahead, it looks like Black has a draw. Mr. Vair proves otherwise.

Problem No. 62

White to Play and Win

By L. J. VAIR

Our fourth and final position by the "Kolorado Kowboy." An amusing little fellow that will prove entertaining to all grades of players.

Problem No. 63

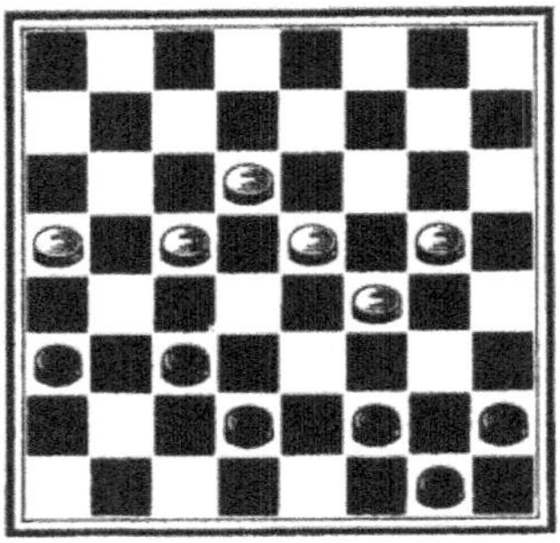

Black to Play and Win

By JESSE B. HANSON

The author of Problems No. 63–66 is one of America's greatest living players. He has been for many years the Pacific Coast Champion and was a member of the victorious All-American team in 1927. He has also been a major prize winner in quite a few National tournies and on one occasion reached the final round. He has published numerous problems of a very high order. Number 63 is a good example of his work.

By JESSE B. HANSON

Number 64 has some very nice points and was won by the author in a match game some years back.

Problem No. 64

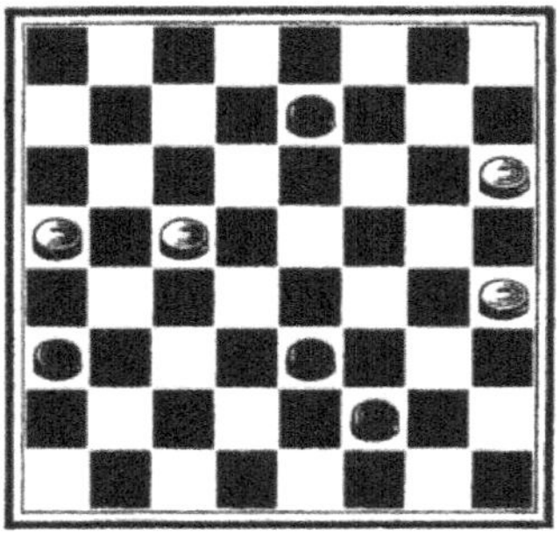

Black to Play and Win

Problem No. 65

Black to Play and Draw

By JESSE B. HANSON

Here is a nice little study in correct timing. The slightest mismove on Black's part and White is sure to score.

Problem No. 66

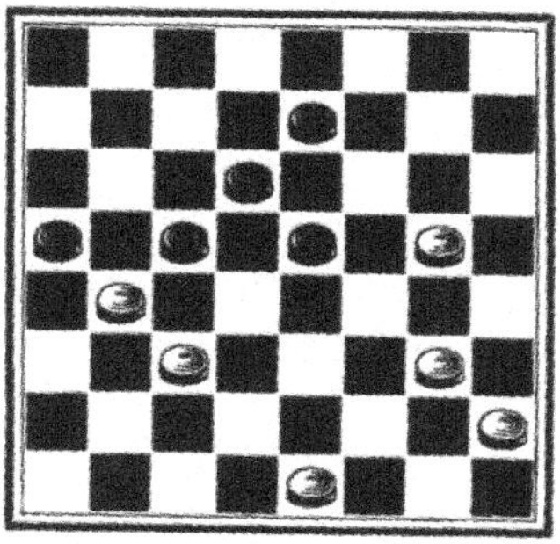

White to Play and Win

By JESSE B. HANSON

We got a lot of pleasure out of solving Problem No. 66 and don't mind admitting that we found it difficult. Nevertheless we felt that our time had been well spent as Mr. Hanson unfolds some beautiful play in this one.

Problem No. 67

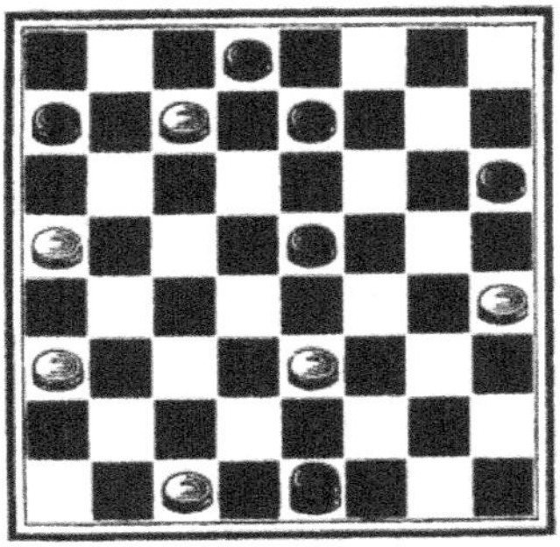

White to Play and Draw

By PAUL R. SEMPLE

The author of positions No. 67–70 is one of America's foremost problem composers and a leading player of the state of Ohio. Mr. Semple, who is a native of Martin Ferry, is an amateur magician and a master at performing tricks on the checker board. Problem No. 67 is a good example of his work.

By PAUL R. SEMPLE

Positions No. 67 and 68 are companion problems and illustrate an unusually pretty drawing theme that is well worth noting. Number 68 has proved a stumbling block to many strong players.

Problem No. 68

White to Play and Draw

Problem No. 69

White to Play and Win

By PAUL R. SEMPLE

Problem No. 69 is a very neat 3 by 3 that requires exact play. This idea is one that frequently arises in actual crossboard games.

Problem No. 70

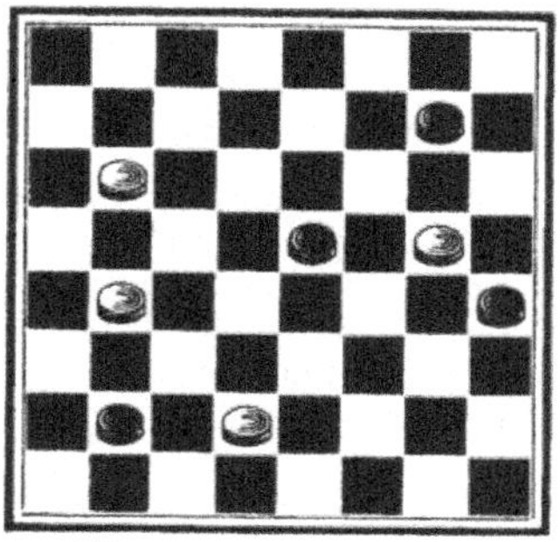

White to Play and Draw

By PAUL R. SEMPLE

Problem No. 70 looks like a very natural ending rather than a composed position. It demonstrates one of the themes treated in our end-game section. Very nice, Mr. Semple.

Problem No. 71

White to Play and Draw

By LOUIS C. GINSBERG

Two of the greatest players of the modern era were natives of Brooklyn—Gonotsky and Ginsberg. The latter was a member of the 1927 International Match and was runner-up to Asa Long in the 7th American Tourney at Cedar Point, Ohio. He is also a noted lecturer and author and his booklet on the Dyke is considered one of the finest treatises ever published on the game.

By LOUIS C. GINSBERG

Here is a neat little position that has appeared in a number of columns during the past few years. This is the type of win that many players overlook nine times out of ten.

Problem No. 72

White to Play and Win

Problem No. 73

Black to Play and Win

By NORMAN CLARK

Numbers 73 and 74 are by the Checker Editor of the Bangor Commercial. Mr. Clark is one of Maine's leading players and is well known throughout the country as an analyst and problem composer. Many fine corrections of published play by this critic have already appeared in print.

Problem No. 74

Black to Play, White Wins

By NORMAN CLARK

Though not very difficult, it is one that the beginner might easily overlook.

Problem No. 75

White to Play and Draw

By WILLIAM J. WOOD

Mr. Wood, the problem King of the National Checker Association, has published many fine end-games and problems in checker periodicals all over the world. He is a native of Waukeegan, Ill. and a neighbor of another famous problemist, Charles Hefter of Kankakee. All experts are familiar with Mr. Wood's fine analysis on various phases of First Position.

By WILLIAM J. WOOD

There is quite a snap to this one so be careful you don't get bitten. It is no doubt that problems like this earned Mr. Wood the title of Problem King.

Problem No. 76

White to Play and Win

Problem No. 77

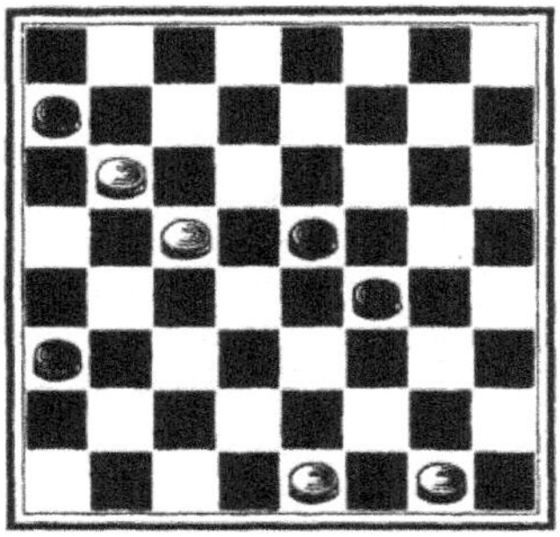

White to Play and Win

By JACK GORDON

Brooklyn seems to have produced more famous checker players and problemists than any city in America. Gonotsky, Ginsberg, Nelson, Boland and Jack Gordon are only a few of the Brooklynites who have distinguished themselves in the checker world. Mr. Gordon's problems are often very deep and are of the type more appreciated by the advanced player rather than the student. We have selected two of his easier problems that are more suitable for the average player.

Problem No. 78

White to Play and Win

By JACK GORDON

Though the reader may think otherwise, there is only one way to win Problem No. 78. Don't be hasty with this one. It is a real "fooler."

Problem No. 79

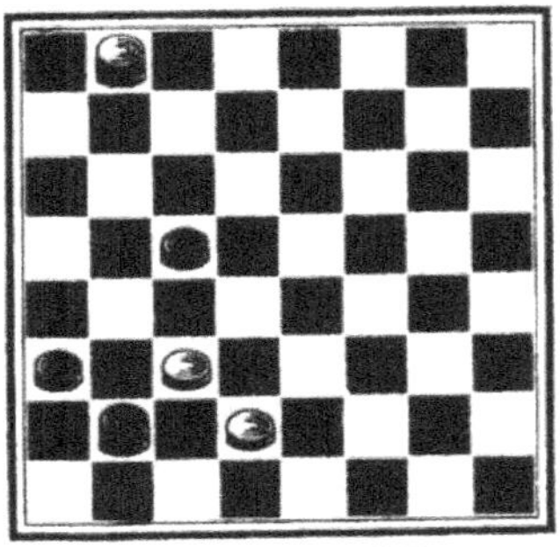

White to Play and Draw

By JAMES MOIR

Mr. Moir, who comes from a famous family of checker players is the Checker Editor of the Hartford Courant and one of the leading promoters of the game in Connecticut. Problem No. 79 is one the student will surely find to his liking.

By JAMES MOIR

After a few forcing moves in No. 80, White springs a trap that ends the game in fine style. A spectacular finish that came up in actual play.

Problem No. 80

White to Play and Win

Problem No. 81

White to Play and Draw

By E. J. REES

The author of Nos. 81 and 82 was formerly a resident of Flint, Michigan but now lives in Llanelly, Wales where he edits a fine checker column in the Llanelly Star. Mr. Rees is a very strong player, the Champion of Wales.

Problem No. 82

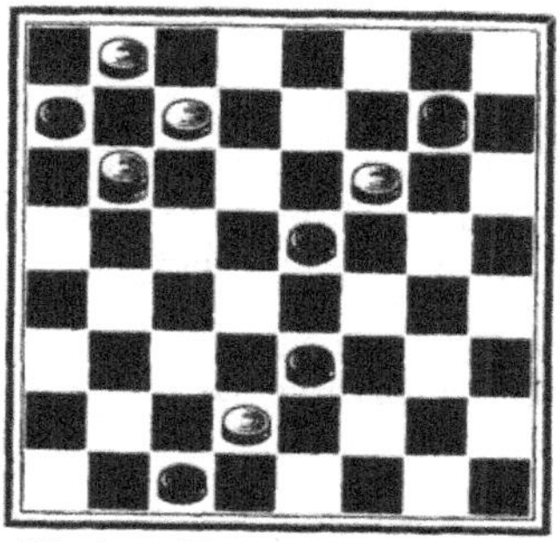

Black to Play, White to Draw

By E. J. REES

Mr. Rees shows some very beautiful play in No. 82 that is sure to please all grades of players. Plenty of "fire works" in this one.

Problem No. 83

Black to Play and Draw

By HOWARD W. STUBBLEBINE

Problem No. 83 is a nice original position by one of Pennsylvania's leading players. White loses a man but gets it back and draws the game by correct play.

Problem No. 84

White to Play and Draw

AUTHOR UNKNOWN

This little gem was clipped from the columns of the Roseville Citizen. The Checker Editor states that it puzzled the best players in Chicago, and that is not surprising as it is really "catchy."

Problem No. 85

Black to Play and Draw

By JOHN G. FINLEY

An ending that came up a few years back between Mr. Finley, a former Champion of New Jersey and Tom LaRacy, present Skeeter State Title holder. Mr. Finley is the Checker Editor of the Roseville (New Jersey) Citizen and one of the leading promoters of checkers in America.

By J. K. BATESON and W. HALLIWELL

Position No. 86 appears in Gould's Problem Book (No. 1004) as a draw. The author is T. B. Murphy. Messrs. Bateson and Halliwell show that by correct play White can win. This position was contributed by Mr. Bateson of Stockport, England, President of the English Draughts Association.

Problem No. 86

White to Play and Win

Problem No. 87

White to Play and Win

By ARNOLD GALLUB

We set No. 87 up for several strong New York players and they all got it—on the second attempt. The author, a popular young Gotham player, says the only hard thing about this position is doing it the first time. We agree.

By VINCENT CONNOLLY

The author, a well known New York player, drew this fine ending in a recent New York Masters' Tournament. A very nice piece of timing.

Problem No. 88

White to Play and Draw

Problem No. 89

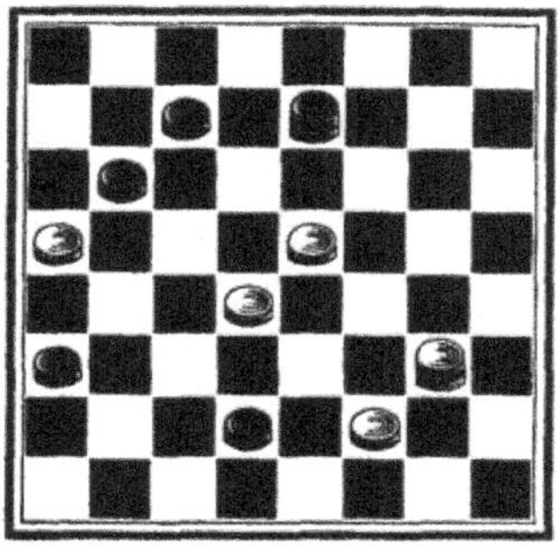

White to Play and Win

By BARNEY TALIS

Problem No. 89 was contributed by the author who states that he won it in the 1938 Chicago Masters' Tournament. What a shock for poor Black.

By BERT BERRY

The author of No. 90 is probably America's most prolific composer of checker problems. Mr. Berry, who hails from Lincoln, Nebraska is well known to checker players the world over as the originator of hundreds of fine problems. He is a frequent contributor to such periodicals as The Roseville Citizen, Mt. Sterling Advocate, Woods Checker Player and The American Checkerist.

Problem No. 90

White to Play and Win

Problem No. 91

Black to Play and Draw

By HAROLD M. FREYER

Number 91 is a fine piece of analysis by the former Junior Champion of America. Although the author is but 21 years of age, he is considered one of the greatest players in America today.

By MILTON LOEW and TOMMIE WISWELL

This ending came up between Mr. Loew and another player in a recent New York Tourney. The draw was missed in the actual game and the authors discovered it shortly afterwards while having "coffee and cake" together. Mr. Loew, who is but 16 years of age, is the present U. S. Junior Champion and one of New York's ten best players.

Problem No. 92

White to Play and Draw

Problem No. 93

White to Play and Win

By IRVING DAVIDS

The author of No. 93 is a well known Pacific Coast player and a native of San Diego, California. His numerous instructive positions have a special appeal to the student.

Problem No. 94

White to Play and Win

By FRED L. WILLIAMS, JR.

Number 94 is an ending the author won from Webster Skelton when the latter was Champion of Georgia. Mr. Williams is Checker Editor of the Atlanta Journal and one of the leading promoters of the game in the Southland.

Problem No. 95

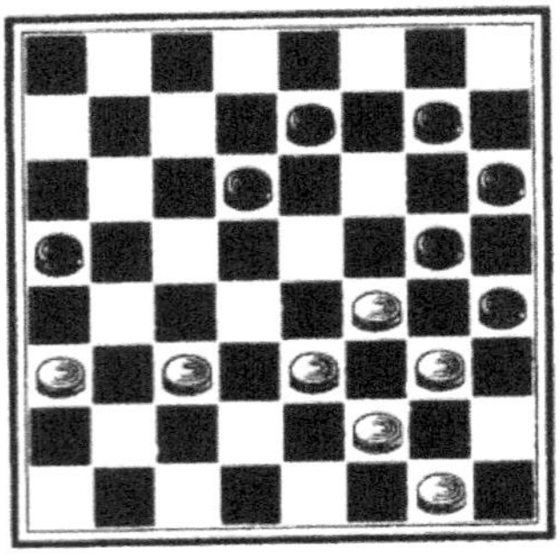

White to Play and Win

By EDWIN F. HUNT

Problem No. 95 is a very nice correction of published play by one of America's Grandmasters. Mr. Hunt, who hails from Tennessee, is a former American Champion and was at one time a leading contender for the world's championship. In a match with Asa Long for this title, he lost by the close score of 3-1 and 35 draws.

By A. J. MANTELL

Position No. 96 arose between Hugh Henderson and Alfred Jordan in the 1915 American Tourney. At this stage, Henderson played 9-14 and although he managed to win the game, Jordan missed a draw as pointed out by the annotater, N. W. Banks. Mr. Mantell, the famous analyst shows how White could have forced the win.

Problem No. 96

White to Play and Win

Problem No. 97

White to Play and Win

By FRANK A. MILLER

The author of No. 97 is a former Champion of the state of Washington and is Checker Editor of the Seattle Star. This is another setting of a theme that we have treated elsewhere in the problem section. Mr. Miller is well known as a problemist and has made a special study of midget problems—(two by twos —a field that was nearly exhausted in the early days by such pioneers as the famous Dr. Brown).

By REX B. WOOD

Mr. Wood is a Pioneer in the publishing field and is at present Editor and Publisher of the monthly magazine, Wood's Checker Player. This contribution is an ending from actual play.

Problem No. 98

White to Play and Draw

Problem No. 99

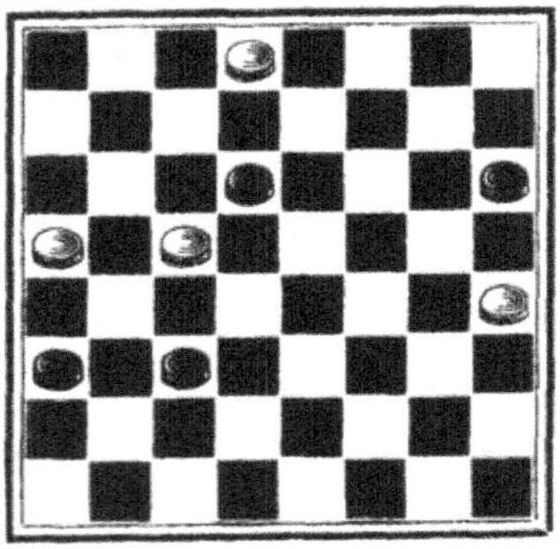

Black to Play and Draw

By WILLIAM F. RYAN

The author of No. 99 is the National Checker Association Champion and Editor of the American Checkerist. He is also the author of numerous textbooks on the game and is one of the country's leading exhibition players. Mr. Ryan formerly held the World's Championship at blindfold checkers.

By KENNETH M. GROVER

Our final selection is an interesting study by the co-author of "Let's Play Checkers."

Problem No. 100

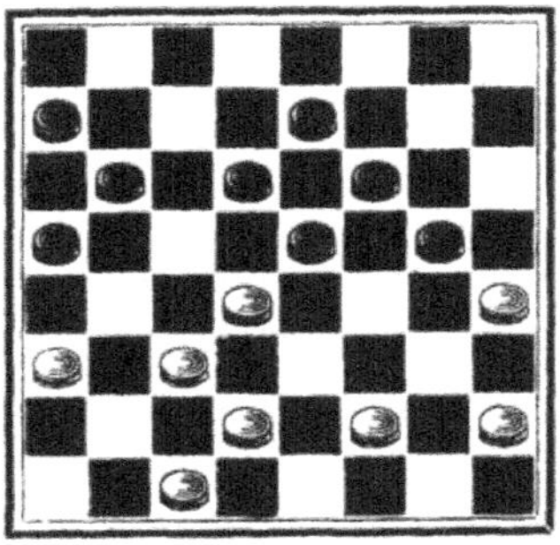

White to Play and Win

PROBLEM SOLUTIONS

Solutions to problems by Tommie Wiswell

No. 1—13-9, 22-26, 29-25, 26-30, 25-21, 30-26, 21-17, 26-23, 17-13, 23-19, 9-6, 2-9, 13-6, 19-15, 6-2, 15-8, 2-7, etc. Drawn.

No. 2—29-25, 14-17 (Best), 25-21, 17-22, 15-18, 22-25, 31-27, 25-30, 27-24, 12-16 (If 30-26, 18-22. Drawn), 24-20, 16-19, 20-16, 19-24, 16-11, 24-27, 11-7, 27-31, 7-2, 30-25, 2-7—A, 31-26, 7-11, 26-22, 11-15, 25-29, 18-25, 29-22, 21-17. Drawn.

A. If 2-6, 31-26, 6-10, 25-22, 18-25, 9-14 Black wins.

No. 3—22-17, 14-21, 13-9, 21-17, 9-6, 17-14, 6-2, 14-10, 2-7, 10-6, 7-11, 6-10—A, 12-16, 3-19, 11-15. White wins.

A. If 6-2, 11-16, 2-6, 16-19, 6-10, 12-16, etc. White wins.

No. 4—19-15, 7-14, 6-10, 14-7, 3-10, 17-13, 10-6, 22-17 (21-17, 5-9 same as trunk), 5-9—A, 25-22, 6-2, 13-6, 2-9, 17-13, 9-6 (9-14, 22-17, 15-10, 13-9, etc. Drawn), 21-17, 6-10, 13-9, 10-14, 17-10, 15-13. Black wins.

A. 15-18, 17-14, 18-9, 21-17 only draws.

No. 5—18-14, 21-25, 14-17, 25-30, 17-21, 5-9, 12-8, 9-14, 8-3, 30-26, 3-7, 26-17, 7-10. White wins.

No. 6—13-9, 4-8—A, 9-6, 8-11, 6-2, 11-15, 2-6, 15-18, 31-26, 21-25, 6-10, 25-30, 10-14, 30-23, 32-27, 23-32, 14-23. White wins.

A. Black's only chance to draw is to make a dash for the King row as White threatens to win by holding two pieces (4 and 28) on the side of the board.

No. 7—32-27, 26-19, 27-24, 20-27, 31-15, 6-9, 14-10, 9-14, 15-11!!, 8-6, 17-1. White wins.

No. 8—24-20, 32-16, 20-11, 13-17 (If 6-10, 25-22 White wins handily), 11-8!!—A, 6-13, 8-3, 2-6, 3-7, 6-9, 7-11, 9-14, 11-16, 14-18, 16-19, 17-22, 19-15, 22-29, 15-22. White wins.

A. 9-5, 6-9, 5-1, 9-14, 1-5, 14-18, 5-9, 2-6, 9-2, 17-22. Drawn.

No. 9—18-14, 11-16, 1-6, 15-19, 6-9—A, 19-24, 9-6, 24-31, 6-10, 31-22, 23-19, 16-23, 14-9, 5-14, 10-19. Drawn.

A. If 6-10 or 6-1 Black wins by 5-9, 14-5, 19-24 and two White men must go.

No. 10—31-27 (If 9-14, 23-27, etc. will draw), 23-26, 30-23, 13-17, 9-14, 17-22, 14-18, 22-26, 18-22, 26-31, 27-24!!, 20-27, 23-19. White wins.

No. 11—14-10—A, 22-13, 10-6, 2-9, 15-10, 7-14, 16-11, 13-17, 23-18, etc. White wins.

A. If 15-11, 22-13, 23-19, 13-17, 14-9, 3-8!! Well Drawn.

No. 12—11-7, 26-19 (If 2-11, 9-6, etc. drawn as in trunk), 9-6, 2-11 (or 2-9), 18-15, 11-18, 10-7, 1-10, 17-14, 10-17, 21-14, 3-17, 30-16. Drawn.

Solutions to problems by Charles Hefter

No. 13—6-9, 7-10, 19-23, 10-14, 13-17, 8-11, 23-26, 11-15, 26-22 14-10, 9-13, 21-14, 13-17. Black wins.

No. 14—1-6, 7-11, 6-10, 23-19, 9-13, 15-18, 10-15, 19-17, 13-8. White wins.

No. 15—14-9, 18-14, 9-6, 2-9, 13-6, 14-10, 6-2, 10-7, 8-12, 7-16, 2-7. Drawn.

No. 16—9-13, 1-6, 21-25, 23-18, 13-17, 6-10, 17-21 (Threatening to exchange), 18-23, 25-22. Drawn.

No. 17—31-27, 6-9, 27-18, 32-28, 8-11, 28-24, 14-17, 21-14, 18-23. Drawn.

No. 18—23-26, 17-21, 26-30, 31-26, 30-23, 21-30, 23-27, 15-19, 27-32, 19-24, 32-28, 24-27, 28-32, 27-31, 18-23, 31-27, 23-26, 30-23, 22-26, 23-30, etc. Drawn.

No. 19—9-6, 1-10, 5-1, 10-15, 1-6, 14-18, 6-10, 12-16, 7-11, 16-20, 32-28, 20-24, 11-16, 18-23, 16-20, 15-18, 20-27, 23-32, 10-15. Drawn.

No. 20—6-10, 13-9, 3-7, 23-18, 14-23, 9-6, 7-11, 6-2, 23-27, 2-6, 11-15, 19-16, 27-31, 16-11, 10-14, 6-10, 14-18, 10-19, 18-23. Black wins by First Position.

Solutions to problems by Chris Nelson

No. 21—6-9, 30-26, 32-28, 26-31, 9-14, 18-23, 10-15. White wins.

No. 22—10-14, 28-32, 14-9, 32-27, 9-13, 17-22, 26-17, 21-14 13-9. White wins.

No. 23—30-26, 5-9, 13-6, 2-9, 1-6, 9-13, 6-10, 13-17, 10-15, 3-8, 15-18, 17-21, 26-22, 21-25, 22-17, 25-30, 17-14, 30-25, 14-10, 8-12, 10-7, 16-19, 7-3, 26-31, 3-7, 31-27, 7-11, 27-32, 28-24, 19-28, 18-23. White wins.

No. 24—21-17, 26-30, 14-10, 23-26—A, 7-11, 26-31, 17-14, 31-26, 22-18, 26-22—B, 11-15, 30-26, 10-6, 22-17, 14-10, 26-23, 18-14, 17-22, 15-18. Drawn.

A. 23-19—B, 17-14, 19-24, 22-18, 30-26, 10-6, 26-23, 7-11, 24-19, 11-7, 13-17, 6-9, 23-26, 9-13, 17-21, and 14-10. Drawn.

B. 30-25, 10-6, 25-18, 7-10, 13-22, 6-9. Drawn.

No. 25—3-7, 29-25, 7-2, 13-9, 5-1, 25-22, 1-6, 9-5, 2-7, 5-1, 6-9, 14-18, 7-3, 1-5, 9-14, 18-23, 14-9, 5-14, 15-11. White wins.

No. 26—15-19, 24-27, 22-26, 27-31, 18-14, 9-27, 26-22. White wins.

No. 27—11-15, 20-24, 15-19, 24-28, 19-24, 28-32, 24-28, 32-27, 14-18, 12-16, 18-15, 27-32, 28-24, 32-28, 15-11, 28-19, 11-20. White wins. The regular First Position play will not win in this problem—C. Nelson.

No. 28—6-9, 14-17, 9-13, 17-22, 1-6, 23-19, 13-9, 11-15, 9-14, 22-26, 6-10, 26-30, 3-7, 30-26, 7-11. White wins.

Solutions to problems by Ben Boland

No. 29—10-14—A, 26-22, 14-9, 22-18, 21-17, 18-22, 17-14, 8-11, 14-10, 22-18, 10-7, 11-15, 7-2—16-19, 2-7, 19-23—E, 9-14, 23-32, 14-23, 20-27, 23-26, 12-16—B, 26-22—C, F, 27-31, 7-11, 16-19, 11-18, 19-23. Drawn.

A. 21-17, 26-22, 17-13, 22-17, 13-9, 8-11, 10-7, 11-15, 9-6, 15-18, 7-10, 17-22, 6-1, 18-23. Black wins.

B. 27-31, 7-11. Drawn.

C. 7-10, 27-31, 10-12, 31-22, 28-24—D, 32-27, 24-19, 22-18, 19-16, 27-23, 16-11, 18-15, 11-8, 15-11, 8-4, 11-7, 12-8, 7-3, 8-12, 23-19. Black wins.

D. 12-16, 32-27, 16-19, 22-17, 19-15, 17-14, 15-19, 14-10, 19-16, 10-7. Black wins.

E. J. Wyllie in the Draughts Board, June 1, 1870, No. 131, has a king on 23, his play runs as Note C, but gives it as a draw, overlooking The American Position win.

F. J. P. Reed in No. 38, Hill's Manual, changes Wyllie's position by making a king into a man and plays 7-10, as in Note C, over-looking that 26-22 would draw.

No. 30—10-7, 22-26, 7-2*, 26-30, 2-6, 30-25, 14-10, 25-22, 17-13, 15-11, 6-2, 22-18, 10-7—B, 18-15, 7-3, 8-12, 3-7, 12-16, 13-9—A, 5-14. Drawn.

A. 7-3, 15-10; loses and forms No. 28. R. A. Davis, Stearn's portraits, Vol. 2. Continue; 2-7, 11-2, 20-11. This is now No. 4 in Spayth's Game of Draughts, 1863. Continue: 10-15 (2-6 wins too), 11-8 (3-8, 2-6, 11-7, 6-1. Black wins); 15-11, 8-4, 2-6, 3-8, 5-9. Black wins.

B. 10-6, 18-14, 6-1, 14-9, 13-6, 8-12. Black wins.

No. 31—13-9, 25-30, 9-6—A, 30-26, 6-2, 26-23, 2-7, 23-16, 14-10, 5-9, 10-6, 9-14, 6-1, 14-18, 1-6, 18-23, 6-10, 23-27, 10-14—B, 27-32, 14-18, 32-27, 18-14, 27-23, 14-10—C, 23-19, 10-6, 19-15, 6-9, 15-18, 9-6, 18-14, 6-1, 14-18, 1-6, 18-23, 6-10. Drawn.

A. 14-10, 5-14, 10-7, 30-26, 7-3, 26-31, 3-8, 31-27, 8-15, 27-24, 20-16, 14-18. Black wins.

B. 7-3, 16-19, 3-8, 11-15, 8-11, 12-16, 11-18, 19-23. Black wins.

C. 14-9, 16-19, 7-16, 19-15. Black wins.

No. 32—8-3, 22-18, 3-7, 18-14, 7-11—A, 14-9, 11-8, 9-5, 8-12—B, 5-1, 12-8, 19-15, 8-12, 1-5—C, 12-8, 5-9, 20-16—E, 9-14, 16-11, 14-10, 8-4. Drawn.

A. 7-2, 6-10, 2-7, 19-15, 7-2—D, 15-11, 2-6, 10-15, 6-1, 15-18, 1-5, 11-7, 20-16, 18-22, 16-12, 7-11, 13-9, 14-10, 5-1, 11-7, 12-8, 7-2, etc. Black wins.

B. 8-11, 19-16, 11-8 (if 11-7 or 11-15, 5-1, Black wins), 16-12, 8-11, 5-1. Black wins.

C. 6-9, 13-6, 1-10, 20-16, 15-19, 16-11, 19-15, 11-8. Drawn.

D. 13-9, 14-5, 7-14, 15-19. Black wins.

E. 8-12, 9-14, 12-8, 14-10, 8-12, 10-7, 12-16, 7-3, 16-12, 15-19, 20-16, 19-15. Black wins.

No. 33—24-19, 27-23, 19-15, 3-7, 5-9, 23-18, 15-10, 7-14, 31-26, 14-17, 9-13, 18-22, 26-23, 21-25, 23-18. Drawn.

No. 34—8-3, 31-27, 3-8, 20-24—A, 22-18, 27-23, 26-22, 23-26, 17-14, 26-17, 10-7, 2-11, 8-15, 17-22, 18-14, 22-26, 14-10, 26-23, 10-7, 13-17, 7-3, 17-22, 3-8, 22-26, 8-11, 26-30, 11-8. Drawn.

A. 27-23, 28-24, 20-27, 14-10, etc. Drawn.

No. 35—17-14, 31-26, 14-10, 26-22—A, 10-7, 8-11, 3-8, 11-15, 7-3—B, 15-18—C, 3-7, 22-26, 7-10, 26-23, 8-11, 23-32, 10-15, 20-27, 11-20, 27-31. Drawn.

A. 8-11, 27-23, 20-27, 3-8. White wins.

B. 8-11, 15-18, 11-15, 16-19, 15-10, 19-23, 10-14, 23-32. Black wins.

C. 22-18, 8-11, 16-19, 3-7, 19-23, 7-10, 23-32, 10-19, 20-27, 19-24—D. Drawn.

D. 19-15, 18-23, 11-16, 12-19, 15-31, 23-19. Black wins.

No. 36—26-23, 13-9, 3-8—A, 9-13, 8-12, 13-9, 12-16, 9-13, 16-20, 13-9—B, 23-19—C, 9-13, 20-24, 13-9, 19-16—D, 9-13, 24-27, 13-9, 27-31, 9-13, 31-27, 13-9, 27-24, 9-13, 24-20—E, 13-9, 16-12, 9-13 12-8, 13-9, 8-3, 9-13, 20-16, 13-9, 16-19, 9-13, 19-15, 13-9, 1-5—F 9-14. Drawn.

A. 23-19, 10-7, 3-10, 2-7, 11-2, 9-13. Drawn.

B. 10-7, 1-10, 7-3, 10-14, 3-7, 11-8. Black wins.

C. 20-24, 10-7, 1-10, 7-3, 11-16, 3-7. Drawn.

D. If 19-15, 9-13, Black has to play back to 19, for if 24-27, 10-7, 1-10, 7-3, 10-14, 3-7. Drawn.

E. 16-19, 13-9, 19-15, 9-13, 24-19, 10-7—G, 1-10, 7-3. Drawn.

F. 15-18, 2-7, 11-2, 9-5. Drawn. Or if 3-8, 10-7, 1-10, 7-3, 8-12, 3-7, Drawn.

G. If White now falters and plays 13-9, Black can win by 19-23, 9-14—H, 15-18, 14-9, 1-5, 9-13, 18-14. Black wins.

H. If 10-7—I, 1-10, 7-3, 15-19, Black wins.

I. Or if 9-5—J, 15-18, 5-9, 1-5, Black wins.

J. If 9-13, 23-18, 13-9, 18-14, Black wins.

Above corrects Note to No. 1017 Gould's Problem Book.

Solutions to problems by Fausto Dalumi

No. 37—22-18, 23-27, 18-23, 27-32, 24-20, 9-14, 20-11, 14-10, 23-19, 32-27, 19-16, 27-24, 16-12, 24-19, 12-8, 10-7, 8-12, 7-16, 2-7, 16-20, 12-8, 4-11, 7-23. Drawn.

Note. All White moves of the above solution are starred.

No. 38—7-2, 11-15, 2-6, 15-19, 24-15, 18-4, 6-10, 12-16, 10-15, 4-8, 27-23, 8-12, 15-19. Drawn.

Note. All White moves of the above solution are starred.

No. 39—8-11, 16-20, 11-15, 24-28, 26-23, 20-24—A, 30-26, 28-32, 26-31, 32-27, 15-18, 29-25, 23-19. White wins.

(A) 28-32, 15-19. White wins.

Note. All White moves of the above solution are starred.

No. 40—18-14, 31-26, 23-18, 28-24, 19-15, 26-22, 14-10, 24-19, 18-14, 22-26, 15-11, 19-15, 11-7, 15-6, 7-2, 6-1, 2-6, 1-17, 13-31. White wins.

Note. All White moves of the above solution are starred.

No. 41—19-16, 30-26, 23-19, 26-23, 29-25, 5-9, 25-22, 9-13, 22-25, 1-6, 19-15—A, 23-19, 15-11, 19-12, 25-22, 12-16, 11-7, 16-11, 7-2, 6-10, 2-6, 10-15, 6-10, 15-19, 10-14, 11-15, 14-17. Drawn.

(A) 25-22, 6-10. Black wins.

No. 42—20-16, 6-10, 16-11, 10-15, 11-8, 14-18, 22-17—A, 15-10, 8-4, 18-23, 17-22, 10-15, 4-8, 3-7, 8-4, 23-27, 22-26, 15-19, 12-8. Drawn.

(A) 22-25 loses.

No. 43—20-16, 32-27, 16-11, 10-15, 4-8, 15-22, 30-26, 22-25, 26-23, 27-18, 11-7, 2-11, 8-29. Drawn.

Note. All White moves of the above solution are starred.

No. 44—32-27, 28-32, 27-23, 32-27, 23-18, 27-23, 18-14, 23-18, 14-9, 18-14, 10-7, 13-17—A, 7-3, 17-21, 3-7, 21-25, 7-3, 25-30, 4-8, 14-17, 9-6, 1-10, 3-7, 12-3, 7-21. Drawn.

(A) 14-10, 7-3, 10-15, 4-8, 13-17, 9-6. Drawn.

Note. All White moves of the above solution are starred.

No. 45—10-7, 3-10, 16-11, 15-8, 12-3, 19-23, 3-7, 10-15, 7-11, 15-19, 11-16, 19-24, 16-19, 23-26, 19-16, 1-6, 17-14, 26-31, 16-20, 31-26, 20-27, 26-22, 27-23, 22-17, 14-9, 6-13, 23-18. Drawn.

No. 46—17-14, 22-31, 14-10, 6-9, 15-11, 9-14—A, 19-23, 14-17, 23-18, 31-26, 10-6—B, 2-9, 11-7, 3-10, 18-23, 26-19, 24-22. White wins.

(A) 31-26, 10-7. White wins.

(B) 18-22 only draws. All White's moves are starred.

Solutions to problems by A. J. Heffner

No. 47—31-26, 8-11, 14-10, 6-15, 32-27, 19-24, 28-12, 11-16, 12-8, 15-19, 23-18, 19-24, 27-23, 24-27, 18-15, 27-31, 15-11, 31-22, 23-18, 22-15, 8-3, 15-8, 3-19. White wins.

No. 48—1-5, 29-25, 5-9, 25-22, 9-13, 22-18, 30-26, 21-25, 13-9, 25-30, 9-5, 30-23, 32-27, 23-32, 10-6, 2-9, 5-23. White wins.

No. 49—13-9, 8-11—A, 9-5—B, 12-8, 5-1, 8-12, 1-5—C, 12-8, 5-1, 8-3, 20-16—D, 11-20, etc. Drawn.

A. 10-14, 18-15, 14-18, 20-16. Drawn.

B. 9-6, 11-15, 18-11, 12-8 jump either way, then 21-25. Black wins.

C. 1-6 allows win same as in B after 9-6.

D. 1-5, 21-25, 5-1, 10-15, 1-6, 15-19, 6-10, 19-23, 10-6, 23-26, 6-10, 26-31. Black wins—A. J. Heffner.

No. 50—16-20, 31-27, 23-18, 14-23, 19-24, 26-31, 32-28, 23-26, 28-32, 27-23, and 24-27. White wins.

No. 51—11-7—A, 31-26—C, 17-14, 6-9, 7-2, 9-13, 2-7—D, 26-22—E, 7-10, 22-29, 21-17, 13-22, 14-9, 5-14, 10-26, 29-25, 26-22, etc. Drawn.

A. 17-13—B, 31-26, 21-17, 26-22, 25-21, 18-23, 11-7, 22-18, 7-3, 23-26, 3-7, 26-30, 7-11, 30-26, 11-16, 26-23, 16-11, 23-19, 17-14, 18-9, 21-17, 19-23, 11-15, 6-10. Black wins.

B. 17-14, 6-9, 11-7, 9-13, 14-10, 31-26, etc. Black wins.

C. 6-9, 17-13, 9-14, 7-2. Drawn.

D. 2-6, 26-23, 6-10, 18-22, 25-18, 5-9. Black wins.

E. 26-23, 14-10. Draws—A. J. Heffner.

No. 52—32-28, 11-15—A, 22-17, 15-24, 28-19, 14-18, 30-26, 18-23, 26-22, 23-26, 22-18, 26-31, 18-15, 31-27, 15-6, 2-9, 17-13, 9-14, 25-22, 7-10, 16-11, 27-24, 19-15, 10-19, 11-7, 24-27, 7-2, 27-31, 2-6, 31-26, 6-9, 26-17, 9-18. Drawn.

A. 2-6—C, 30-26, 11-15—B, 26-23, 15-24, 28-19, 20-24, 22-17, etc. Drawn.

B. 6-9, 26-23, 9-13, 22-18, 14-17, 21-14, 10-17, 25-22, 17-26, 19-15, 12-19, 23-16. Drawn.

C. 14-17, 22-13, 20-24, 25-22, 11-20, 22-18, 7-11, 18-14, 10-17, 21-14, 24-27, 30-25, 27-31, 25-22, 31-26, 22-18, 26-22, 19-15, 11-16, 14-10, 20-24, 28-19, 16-23, 10-6, 2-9, 13-6, 23-27, 6-2, etc. Drawn.

Solutions to problems by Samuel Gonotsky

No. 53—13-9, 12-16, 9-6, 10-15, 6-2, 19-23, 2-7, 23-32, 7-10, 16-19, 10-14, 18-23, 25-22. Drawn.

No. 54—26-22, 19-26, 14-18, 15-19, 18-23, 24-27, 31-15, 26-31, 22-18, 31-27, 15-11*, 30-25, 23-26. Drawn.

No. 55—28-24, 1-6, 14-10, 6-15, 25-21, 3-8, 17-14, 8-12, 21-17, 15-19, 24-8, 16-19, 23-16, 12-19, 8-3, 19-23, 14-10, 23-32, 10-6, 32-27, 18-15, 27-23, 15-11, 20-24, 6-1, 24-27, 3-7, 27-31, 7-10*, 31-27, 10-6, 27-24, 11-7, 24-19, 7-2, 19-15, 2-7. Drawn.

No. 56—21-17, 15-19, 17-14, 1-6, 14-9, 6-10, 9-6, 10-14, 6-2, 14-17, 11-7, 3-10, 32-27, 24-31, 2-7. Drawn.

No. 57—24-19, 7-11, 19-16, 12-19, 27-24, 20-27, 31-6, 2-9, 1-5, 11-16, 5-1, 16-19, 1-6, 14-17, 22-18, 17-21, 6-10, 13-17, 10-15, 19-23, 18-14, 9-18, 15-13. Drawn.

No. 58—2-6, 22-26, 6-9, 26-31, 9-18, 31-27, 30-26, 27-31, 18-22, 31-27, 22-13, 27-18, 26-22, 18-25, 13-17. Drawn.

Solutions to problems by L. J. Vair

No. 59—10-7, 20-24, 3-8, 11-4, 22-17, 21-14, 7-10, 14-7, 2-27. White wins.

No. 60—24-19, 15-24, 20-27, 32-23, 1-5, 9-14—A, 25-22, 18-25, 5-9, 13-6, 2-27. White wins.

A. 18-22, 25-18, 23-14, 2-6. White wins.

No. 61—9-6, 1-10, 5-1, 20-24—A, 1-6, 10-15, 13-9, 22-13, 6-1, 13-6, 1-28. White wins.

A. 10-15, 13-9, 22-6, 1-19. White wins. Or 20-16, then 1-6 and again White drives Black into the 3 for 2.

No. 62—22-26, 12-16, 28-24, 19-28, 26-23, 16-20, 31-27. White wins.

Solutions to problems by Jesse B. Hanson

No. 63—6-10, 17-13, 10-17, 18-14, 5-9—A, 14-5, 7-10, 23-18, 17-22, 13-9, 22-26, 9-6, 26-31, 6-2, 31-26, 18-15, 11-18, 2-7, 10-14, 7-10, 18-22, 10-17, 26-31, 17-26, 31-22, 19-15, 12-16, 20-11, 22-18. Black wins.

A. 17-22, 23-18, 5-9, 13-6, 1-17, 19-15. Drawn.

No. 64—26-31, 20-16, 10-14, 16-11, 6-10, 11-7, 31-27, 7-2, 27-24, 2-6, 24-15, 6-9, 14-18, 21-17, 12-16, 9-14, 15-11, 14-23, 11-15, 23-27, 16-19, 27-32, 19-23. Black wins.

No. 65—5-1, 3-8, 2-7, 8-3, 7-10, 22-17, 1-6, 24-20, 6-2, 20-16, 15-19, 16-11, 10-15, 3-7, 15-18, 7-10, 19-24, 10-15, 18-22. Drawn.

No. 66—24-19, 14-21, 28-24, 21-25, 31-27, 25-30, 27-23, 13-17, 22-13, 30-26, 13-9, 26-31, 9-6, 31-27, 6-2, 27-11, 2-6, 15-24, 6-8, 24-27, 8-3, 7-10, 23-18. 27-31. 3-7. White wins.

Solutions to problems by Paul R. Semple

No. 67—23-18, 15-22, 13-9, 5-14, 30-26, 2-9, and 26-3. Drawn.

No. 68—17-14, 10-17, 21-14, 18-22, 14-9!, 1-5, 24-19!, 15-31, 30-26, 5-14, 26-1. Drawn.

No. 69—21-17, 25-29, 17-13, 3-7, 12-8, 7-10, 8-3, 10-15, 3-7, 15-18, 7-10, 18-23, 10-14, 22-26—A, 14-17, 26-31, 30-25. White wins.

A. 23-27, 13-9, 27-31, 14-17. White wins.

No. 70—16-11, 8-12, 26-22, 25-30, 17-13, 30-25, 22-17, 25-21, 17-14, 21-17, 14-10, 17-14, 11-7, 14-5, 13-9, 5-14, 7-3, 14-7, 3-19 etc. Drawn.

Solutions to problems by Louis C. Ginsberg

No. 71—3-7, 28-24, 11-8, 24-19, 8-4, 10-15, 4-8, 14-18, 8-11, 19-24, 7-10, 15-19, 11-16, 18-23, 16-20, 23-27, 20-16, 19-23, 16-19, 24-15, 10-26. Drawn.

No. 72—23-18, 9-5, 18-14, 5-1, 19-15, 12-16, 15-11, 16-20, 11-8, 20-24, 8-3, 1-5, 3-7, 6-10, 14-17, 10-15, 7-11, 15-18, 11-15, 18-23 White wins.

Solutions to problems by Norman Clark

No. 73—6-9, 13-6, 2-9, 29-25, 9-14, 25-21, 12-16, 11-8—A, 14-10, 20-11, 19-16, 8-12, 16-7, 12-16, 10-15, 21-17, 7-10. Black wins.

A. 21-17, 14-21, 11-8, 21-17, 20-11, 17-14, 8-3, 14-10, 11-8, 19-16, 8-4, 16-12. Black wins.

No. 74—25-22, 27-24, 22-15, 31-27, 15-18, 19-16, 11-20, 27-32, etc. White wins.

Solutions to problems by Wm. J. Wood

No. 75—8-3, 25-30, 3-10, 30-26, 9-6, 26-17, 6-2, 17-22, 10-14, 22-26, 14-10, 26-31, 2-7, 31-27, 7-11. Drawn.

No. 76—25-21, 6-10, 27-23, 12-16, 20-11, 10-15, 21-17, 15-22, 23-18, 22-26, 17-14, 13-17, 14-5. White wins.

Solutions to problems by Jack Gordon

No. 77—32-27, 21-25, 9-6, 25-30, 6-2, 30-25, 2-6, 25-22, 6-10, 22-18, 14-9, 5-14, 10-17, 19-23, 17-14, 23-32, 14-23, 32-28, 31-26, 28-32, 26-22, etc. White wins by stealing the Black piece on 15 after crowning piece on 22.

No. 78—15-10, 28-32, 23-19, 32-28, 10-7, 17-22, 19-23, 28-32, 7-3, 22-17, 23-19, 32-28, 3-7, 17-22, 7-10, 22-17, 10-15, 17-22, 15-18—A. White wins.

A. The only way this position can be won—Jack Gordon.

Solutions to problems by James Moir

No. 79—1-6, 25-18, 6-9, 14-17, 9-13, 18-22, 26-23, 21-25, 23-18. Drawn.

No. 80—9-6, 1-5, 13-9, 10-15, 7-10, 14-7, 6-2, 5-14, 2-9. White wins.

Solutions to problems by E. J. Rees

No. 81—26-23, 32-28, 20-16, 15-19, 23-18, 19-23, 21-17!! Drawn.

No. 82—10-15, 7-2, 25-21, 27-23, 18-25, 23-19, 15-18, 2-7, 3-10, 19-15. Drawn.

Solutions to problems by various authors

No. 83—8-11, 23-16, 11-20, 30-25, 7-11, 25-22, 11-15, 22-13, 14-18, 13-9, 15-19, 9-6, 20-24, 6-2, 24-27, 2-7, 27-31. Drawn.

No. 84—12-8, 13-17, 8-3, 17-22, 16-12, 22-26, 12-8, 26-31, 11-7, 4-11, 7-2, etc. Drawn.

No. 85—14-18, 2-6, 10-14, 6-10 (If 6-9, 18-23 Black wins), 31-27, 10-17, 27-24, 17-14, 24-15, 14-23 and 15-19. Drawn.

No. 86—24-28, 20-16—A, 2-7, 16-11, 7-16, 12-19, 6-10, 19-23—B, 28-24, 23-26, 10-14, 26-30—C, 24-19, 30-25, 14-18, 5-9, 19-23, 9-13, 23-26, 13-17, 26-30, 25-21, 18-22, 17-26, 30-23. White wins.

A. 12-16, 2-7, 16-19, 7-11, 19-23, 11-15, 23-26, 15-19, 26-30, 28-32, 30-25, 32-27, 25-22, 27-23, 22-17, 23-26, 17-13, 26-22, 5-9, 22-18. White wins.

B. 5-9, 10-15, 19-23, 28-24, 9-13, 15-18, 23-26, 24-28, 26-31, 18-23, 13-17, 23-27, 31-24, 28-19. White wins.

C. 26-31, 14-18, 31-26, 24-28, 5-9, 28-24, 9-13, 24-28, 26-31, 18-23, 13-17, 23-27, 31-24, 28-19. White wins.

No. 87—29-25—A, 21-30, 27-23, 20-27, 12-8, 4-11, 10-15, 11-18, 23-21. White wins.

A. If 27-23, 20-27, 23-30, 17-14, etc. Drawn.

No. 88—22-17, 13-22, 26-17, 24-27, 31-24, 20-27, 17-13, 27-31, 9-6, 2-9, 13-6, 31-27, 6-2, 27-24 (If 27-23, 11-8 Drawn) 19-16, 12-19, 2-7. Drawn.

No. 89—18-14, 9-18, 13-9, 6-13, 27-23, 18-27, 24-22. White wins.

No. 90—16-11, 28-24, 19-15, 24-19, 15-10, 19-15, 11-7, 15-6, 30-25!, 21-30, 7-2, 30-23, 2-27. White wins.

No. 91—15-19, 1-6, 10-15, 6-10, 11-16, 10-7—A, 15-18, 7-11—B, 16-20, 11-16—C, 18-22, 32-28—E, 19-24, 28-19, 23-27, 31-24, 20-27, 16-20 (16-11, 27-32, 11-15, 32-28), 27-32, 20-24, 32-28, 24-27, 28-32, 27-31, 32-28, 19-15, 28-32, 15-10, 12-16, 10-6, 16-20, 6-1, 32-27, 31-24, 20-27, 1-6, 27-32, 6-10, 32-27. Drawn.

A. 10-14—D, 23-27, 32-23, 19-26, 30-23, 16-20. Drawn.

B. 30-25, 19-24, 32-28, 23-27, 28-19, 16-23, 31-24, 12-16, 24-20, 16-19, 7-11, 23-26, 11-15, 26-30. Drawn.

C. 31-26—G, 12-16, 11-15, 20-24, 15-22, 24-27, 32-28, 16-20. Drawn.

D. 31-26, 15-18, 10-15—F, 18-22, 26-17, 16-20, 15-24, 20-27. Drawn.

E. 32-27 (31-27 allows 22-26, 27-18, 19-24, 30-23, 12-26. Black wins.), 23-32, 16-23, 12-16, etc. Drawn.

F. 32-28, 16-20, 10-14, 20-24, 14-10, 24-27, 10-15, 27-31, 15-22, 23-27, 26-23, 19-26, 30-23. Drawn.

G. 11-15, 18-22, 15-24, 20-27, 31-24, 12-16, 24-19, 16-20, 19-15. Drawn.

No. 92—19-23, 24-27 (24-19 is no better), 23-19, 27-31, 19-23, 12-16, 11-20, 31-27, 20-16, 27-18, 16-19, 18-14, 19-23. Drawn.

No. 93—15-11, 21-17, 14-10, 17-14, 9-6, 14-16, 8-12, 2-9, 12-26. White wins.

No. 94—11-15, 20-24, 15-18, 24-20, 18-14, 17-22, 14-10—A, 20-24, 10-15, 22-26, 30-23, 24-27, 23-19. White wins.

A. 14-18, 22-26, 30-23, 31-27, 32-28—B, 20-16. Drawn.

B. 23-19, 20-24. Black wins.

No. 95—32-28, 8-11, 22-18, 13-17, 21-14, 10-17, 19-15, 16-19, 23-16, 12-19, 15-8, 19-23, 24-19, 23-32, 8-3. White wins.

No. 96—9-13, 23-32, 29-25, 22-29, 13-15, 12-16, 15-18, 16-19, 18-22, 32-27, 3-8, 27-31, 22-18, 31-27, 8-12, 19-23, 28-24, 27-32, 18-27, 32-23, 24-19. White wins.

No. 97—26-22, 18-25, 15-11, 5-9, 11-7, 4-8—A, 7-2, 8-12, 2-6, 9-14, 21-17, 14-21, 6-10, 12-16, 10-15. White wins.

A. 9-14, 21-17, 14-21, 7-3. White wins.

No. 98—7-2, 1-6, 9-5, 6-9, 14-10, 15-6, 5-1, 6-10, 2-6, etc. Drawn.

No. 99—21-25, 13-9, 25-29, 9-6, 29-25, 6-2, 25-22, 2-7, 22-18, 7-16, 23-27, 31-24, 18-23, 19-15, 12-28. Drawn.

No. 100—26-23, 9-14—A, 18-9, 5-14, 21-17—C, 14-21, 27-24, 10-14—D, 24-19, 15-24, 28-12, 11-15—E, 12-8, 7-10-F, 8-3, 14-17, 22-18—G, 15-22, 23-18, 22-25, 3-7, 25-29, 7-14, 29-25, 18-15. White wins.

A. 10-14, 21-17, 14-21, 27-24, 9-14—B, 18-9, 5-14, 24-19 runs into trunk solution.

B. 7-10, 24-19, 15-24, 28-12, 10-14, 12-8, 14-17, 23-19. White wins.

C. Corrects Tescheleit's Master Play where the following is given to draw: 27-24, 14-17, 21-14, 10-26, 24-19, 15-24, 28-12, 11-15, 23-18, 15-22, 30-23, 7-10, 23-18, 22-26, 12-8, 26-31, 8-3, 31-26. Drawn.

D. Should Black pitch 13-17, 22-13, 15-18, 23-14, 10-17, 13-9, 17-22, 9-6, 22-25, 6-2, 25-30, 2-6, 29-25, 30-26, 25-30, 26-23, 30-25, 23-18 White wins.

E. 7-10, 22-18, 14-17, 23-19. White wins.

F. 7-11, 8-3, 14-17, 22-18, 15-22, 23-19, 22-25, 3-8, 11-16, 19-12, 25-29, 8-11, 29-25, 11-15. White wins.

G. Black secures a neat draw if 30-26, 10-14, 3-7, 21-25—H,

7-11 (If **7-10, 15-18, 22-15, 17-21** Drawn.), **15-19, 23-16, 25-29** and the White man on **22** is gone.

H. If Black attempts a fancy pitch by **15-19** he would lose by this pretty coup: **23-16, 21-25, 7-10, 25-29, 16-11, 17-21, 10-17, 29-25, 26-23, 25-27, 17-22.** White holds the two pieces with his King and wins.

MISCELLANY

THE STANDARD LAWS

LEES' GUIDE RULES REVISED BY JOHN G. FINLEY, AS ADOPTED BY THE AMERICAN CHECKER ASSOCIATION

1. The Official Checker Board of the American Checker Association to be used in National Tournaments and Official Matches shall be of green and buff, two-inch squares. The board shall be placed for playing so that the green Double Corners are on the right-hand side of the players.

2. The Official Checkers of the American Checker Association to be used in National Tournaments and Official Matches shall be turned and round, and of Red and White in color, and of a diameter of not less than one and one-quarter inches, nor more than one and one-half inches. The pieces shall be placed on the Green Squares.

3. At the beginning of a Contest the players shall toss for colors. The first move is made by the player having the Red (called Black in textbooks) pieces. Thereafter, the players shall alternate in leading off with Red in each succeeding opening balloted.

4. At the end of Five Minutes (if the move has not been previously made) "Time" must be called in a distinct manner by the person appointed for that purpose; and if the move is not completed on the expiry of another minute the game shall be adjudged as lost through improper delay. When either player is deaf or partially deaf, a Card on which the word "Time" is printed in large letters shall be placed or laid on the playing table facing the player when it is his time to move.

5. When there are Two or more ways to "Jump," five minutes shall be allowed for the move. When there is only one way to "Jump" Time shall be called at the end of one minute; and if the move is not completed at the expiry of another minute the game shall be adjudged as lost through improper delay.

6. At the beginning of a game each player shall be entitled to arrange his own or his opponent's pieces properly on the squares. After the game has opened (a move has been made) if either player touch or arrange any piece, without giving intimation, he shall be cautioned for the first offense, and shall forfeit the game for any

subsequent offense of this kind. If a person whose turn it is to play touch one of his own playable pieces, he must either play it or forfeit the game.

7. If any part of a playable piece be played over an angle of the square on which it is stationed, the play must be completed in that direction. Inadvertently removing, touching or disturbing from its position a piece that is not playable, while in the act of "jumping" or making an intended move, does not constitute a move, and the piece or pieces shall be placed back in position and the game continued.

8. The "Huff" or "Blow" is hereby abolished. All "jumps" must be completed, and all "jumped" pieces must be removed from the board.

9. When a single piece reaches the crownhead of the board, by reason of a move, or as the completion of a "jump" it becomes a King; and that completes the move, or "jump." The piece must then be crowned by the opponent by placing a piece on top of it. If the opponent neglects to do so and makes a play, then any such play shall be put back until the piece that should have been crowned is crowned. "Time" does not start on the player whose piece should have been crowned until the piece is crowned.

10. A King once crowned, can move in any direction as the limits of the board permit. A King can "jump" in any direction one or more pieces, as the limits of the board permit. When a piece is not available for crowning one must be furnished by the Referee.

11. A Draw is declared when neither player can force a win. When one side appears stronger than the other, and the player with what appears to be the weaker side requests the Referee for a Count on Moves, then, if the Referee so decides, the stronger party is required to complete the win, or show to the satisfaction of the Referee at last an "increased" (instead of the old wording "decided") advantage over his opponent within Forty of his own moves, these to be counted from the point at which notice was given by the Referee; failing in which he must relinquish the game as a draw.

12. After an opening is balloted neither player shall leave the board without permission of the Referee. If permission is granted his opponent may accompany him, or the Referee may designate a person to accompany him. "Time" shall be deducted accordingly from the player whose turn it is to move.

13. Anything that may tend either to annoy or distract the attention of an opponent is strictly forbidden, such as making signs or sounds, pointing, or hovering over the board either with the hands or the head, or unnecessarily delaying to move a piece touched. Any principal so acting, after having been warned of the consequences, and requested to desist, shall forfeit the game.

14. Players shall be allowed to smoke during the conduct of a game, but care must be exercised not to blow smoke across the board, lest it annoy an opponent. If a player is thus annoyed, he may object to his opponent smoking, in which case neither player shall be allowed to smoke.

15. Any spectator giving warning either by signs or sound or remark on any of the games, whether playing or pending, shall be ordered from the room during the contest. Play shall be discontinued until such offending party retires. Spectators shall not be allowed to smoke nor talk near the playing boards.

16. Four games shall constitute a heat or contest. In case of a tie at the end of four games, the players shall continue playing in an effort to break the tie (in two game heats).

17. The Referee shall have full charge of the enforcing of the Rules of the tournament. He shall interpret the Rules and decide all disputes. In the event of an appeal from his decision, he shall immediately call a meeting of the Playing Committee members present, which body shall hear the appeal, discuss the issue involved, and their decision shall be final.

ORGANIZED CHECKERS IN THE UNITED STATES

In 1907 the first tournament for the American Checker Championship was held in Boston, Mass. and was won by the great Charles F. Barker. This initial congress was under the auspices of the newly formed American Checker Association, which body has since held ten such national tournies in all. In recent years, due to a difference in opinion regarding policy, a rival organization has appeared on the scene and is also conducting tournaments for the U. S. championship. This new group is called the National Checker Association and has already held 2 national tournies, one in Providence, R. I. in 1937, and one in Tacoma, Wash. in 1939. We may add that the Authors of this book belong to both organizations.

While it is undoubtedly true that a permanent split in the ranks of the American checker fraternity will do more harm than good, it is nevertheless also true that there has been a distinct increase in activity and interest in the game during the past few years. This is no doubt due in part to the fact that each association is trying to outdo the other in promoting bigger and better tournies. A little more rivalry of this type will not do the game much harm. It is just possible that the American checker officials may learn a lesson from the big baseball moguls. If the National League and the American League, who were formerly bitter rivals, can now work together harmoniously and profitably, maybe the American Checker Association and the National Checker Association can do the same. Let us hope so!

Following is a complete list of the national tournies conducted by both associations, with the names of the winner and runner-up of each:

Championship Tournies Conducted by the A. C. A.

Year		*Venue*	*Winner*	*Runner-Up*
1st	1907	Boston, Mass.	Charles F. Barker	A. J. Heffner
2nd	1912	Cedar Point, O.	Hugh Henderson	H. B. Reynolds
3rd	1915	Chicago, Ill.	Hugh Henderson	Alfred Jordan
4th	1920	Cedar Point, O.	John F. Horr	John T. Bradford
5th	1922	Boston, Mass.	Asa A. Long	Alfred Jordan
6th	1924	New York, N. Y.	Samuel Gonotsky	Alfred Jordan
7th	1929	Cedar Point, O.	Asa A. Long	Louis C. Ginsberg
8th	1934	Jamestown, N. Y.	Edwin F. Hunt	Nathan Rubin
9th	1937	Martins Ferry, O.	Asa A. Long	Willie Ryan
10th	1939	Flint, Mich.	Asa A. Long	Kenneth M. Grover

In 1929, another tournament, purportedly for the American Championship, was staged in Chicago and was won by the champion at that time, Samuel Gonotsky, with Jesse B. Hanson the runner-up.

Championship Tournies Conducted by the N. C. A.

1st	1937	Providence, R. I.	Nathan H. Rubin	Willie Ryan
2nd	1939	Tacoma, Wash.	Willie Ryan	Walter Hallman

Just as important as these national tournies have been the two great international matches between the United States and Great Britain. The first of these affairs was held in Boston and was won by the British by the score of 73 wins, 34 losses, with 284 drawn games. The Americans got revenge in 1927 when the second match was held in New York City and the score was 96 wins to 20 in favor of the home team, with 391 games being drawn.

AMERICA'S TEN BEST ACTIVE PLAYERS

Based upon their records for 1939–1940, we rank the first ten active players of America as follows:

1. Asa Long of Toledo, Ohio (The Iron Man): Number one on our hit parade of American checker favorites is the World's Champion and winner of the recent A. C. A. tourney at Flint, albeit by a very close margin. Incidentally, this was the fourth national tourney in which Mr. Long has emerged victorious. Though it is barely possible that a new name may occupy this favored position next year, until then I believe all parties will agree that Asa is entitled to the honor.

2. Willie Ryan of New York City (The Bronx Comet): A very close second is the winner of the second national tourney of the N. C. A. at Tacoma, and runner up at the 9th tourney at Martins Ferry, Ohio. Mr. Ryan is at present the outstanding contender for the World's title and a worthier candidate would be hard to find. Negotiations are under way for a Long-Ryan match for the World's Championship and should the match be played we feel sure the famous New Yorker will give a good account of himself.

3. Kenneth M. Grover of New York City (The Mighty Mite): Our number three man was runner-up to Long at Flint and tied for third prize at Martins Ferry. He is at present the claimant of the U. S. Eleven Man Title. Grover's playing has been the sensation of the checker world for the past few years and he climaxed his brilliant rise to checker fame at Flint by defeating the World's Champion (1-0-3) in the first heat Mr. Long has lost in 17 years of tourney play. Mr. Grover can be counted on as a serious contender for American and World championship honors.

4 and 5. Walter Hallman of Gary, Ind. (The Gary Gallant): Mr. Hallman is a former Junior Champion of America and has come a long way since he finished in 10th place at the 8th American tourney at Jamestown, N. Y. Walter tied for 3rd prize at the Martins Ferry Tourney in 1937 and just this past summer was runner-up to Ryan at Tacoma. He is another serious contender for American and World's title honors, and possesses as much knowledge of three move play as any player in America. He is well liked and we predict he will score still more impressive victories.

4 and 5. Harold M. Freyer of New York City (The Modern Yates): Mr. Freyer is the former American Junior Champion and

was 3rd prize winner at Flint. Freyer is the third member of this sensational trio (Grover, Hallman, Freyer) that has brought new blood into the game. Freyer's record in the Flint tourney was very impressive. He lost only to one man (Long) and succeeded in defeating the runner-up (Grover) by the score of 1-0 and 11 draws He has won several New York Master Tournies and has the unique record of having tied for first place in three of them (1937, 1938 1939). This young player has not yet reached his peak and it is not hard to picture this likable "kid" as the future American Champion—without the Junior. Our rating for 4th and 5th position was so close we decided to call it a tie.

6. Newell W. Banks of Detroit (The Blindfold Marvel): Mr Banks, who needs no introduction to checker players, is the present World's Blindfold Champion and former U. S. Match Champion He is a veteran campaigner with an impressive list of victories to his credit. Due to an unfortunate break in the recent Tacoma tourney he failed to finish among the first four as everyone had expected, but he played a fine brand of checkers nevertheless, losing only one game throughout the entire tournament. His splendid victory over Sammy Cohen, the English champion, is still fresh in our minds, and we think that the youngsters now coming up so fast will have to contend with this "old timer" for many more years.

7. Lawrence M. Lewis of Chicago (The Speed Demon): A famous player who has returned to the wars after quite a long retirement. He finished in a tie for fourth prize at the Flint tourney and showed by the fine checkers he played that he is still a top notcher. He was one of two men in the tourney who won a game from Asa Long. Mr. Lewis is noted for the speed and accuracy with which he plays, and it is stimulating to see this picturesque celebrity back in the limelight once again.

8. H. B. Reynolds of Buffalo, N. Y. (The Granddaddy of American Checkerists): This list would not be complete without the name of H. B. Reynolds. A prize winner in ten national tournies and a player on both international matches is the record of this grand old player. Just to prove that he is far from through this "Veteran of Veterans" tied for fourth prize at Flint and played a brand of checkers which was the surprise and delight of his many admirers. Look out for this youngster.

9. John T. Bradford of Philadelphia (The Happy Warrior): Our choice for position nine is another survivor of the old school

He was a major prize winner at the Martins Ferry tournament and has won several Chicago Master's tournies recently. He has an imposing record, having been a member of the 1927 (2nd) American international team and was runner-up to John F. Horr in the 4th American tournament. He is one of the leading authorities on three move play and was Editor-in-Chief of the 9th American tournament book. "Brad" has a genial disposition and is very popular with members of the checker fraternity.

10. John B. Stiles of Minneapolis (The "Expert"). We complete our list with the name of a player who is well known to the readers of this book. Mr. Stiles was winner of third prize at Tacoma where he played some great checkers. He is also an acknowledged authority on three move play and is the author of several excellent treatises on this style of play. We do not hesitate to place Mr. Stiles on this "Honor Role" of America's Great.

Note: Some will wonder why Edwin F. Hunt and Nathan Rubin have not been included in this list of America's Great Players. The matter of fact is that both of these masters are in semi-retirement and as this is a ranking of active players only, we felt obliged to omit them from consideration in compiling our list. The same is true of such famous players as Louis C. Ginsberg, Tom J. O'Grady, Jack Cox, Jesse B. Hanson, Harry Lieberman, and several others. It is said that Basil Case plans a comeback and though he did win the Southern tourney this year we hesitate to include his name in this year's ratings. Mr. Case did some great playing in the Seventh American Tourney at Cedar Point, Ohio, but we don't know how he would make out in a national tourney on the three move style today (Wood's Checker Player).

THE PERFECT CHECKER PLAYER

There are times when we like to contemplate that which exists only in the imagination. Recently while in such a frame of mind I drew a mental picture of the Perfect Checker Player. Although we all try to attain as high a degree of proficiency as possible, none of us ever expect to reach the ideal state known as perfection. "The Perfect Checker Player" is purely a legendary figure. With that thought in mind I suggest that the P. C. P. (taking into consideration character, disposition, etc., as well as ability) would probably prossess:

1. The Precision of Asa Long.
2. The Knowledge of Nathan Rubin.
3. The Modesty of Edwin Hunt.
4. The Versatility of Newell Banks.
5. The Confidence of Willie Ryan.
6. The Ingenuity of Louis Ginsberg.
7. The Aptitude of Kenneth Grover.
8. The Profundity of Jack Cox.
9. The Subtlety of Harry Lieberman.
10. The Composure of Jesse Hanson.
11. The Perseverance of Walter Hallman.
12. The Patience of Ray Gould.
13. The Discretion of L. T. deBearn.
14. The Judgment of Charles Hefter.
15. The Perception of A. J. Mantell.
16. The Fortitude of H. B. Reynolds.
17. The Joviality of J. T. Bradford.
18. The Wit of Chris Nelson.
19. The Determination of Harold Freyer.
20. And . . . The Enthusiasm and Love for the game of the average woodpusher.

T. W.